PAINTING WITH
O'Keeffe

PAINTING WITH
O'Keeffe

JOHN D. POLING

TEXAS TECH UNIVERSITY PRESS

This book was set in Aldine. The paper used in this book meets the minimum requirements of ANSI/NISO Z39.48-1992 (R1997). ∞

Design by Tamara Kuciak

Printed in the United States of America

Library of Congress Cataloging-in-Publication Data
    Poling, John D. (John David)
        Painting with O'Keeffe / John D. Poling.
            p.   cm.
        Includes bibliographical references and index.
        ISBN 0-89672-381-X (cloth : alk. paper)
        1. Poling, John D. (John David)—Contributions in painting. 2. O'Keeffe, Georgia, 1887-1986—Appreciation. 3. Artistic collaboration—New Mexico.
    I. Title.
    ND237.P725A2   1999
    759.13—dc21
    [B]   99-10127
                                                                        CIP

00 01 02 03 04 05 06 07 / 9 8 7 6 5 4 3 2

Texas Tech University Press
Box 41037
Lubbock, Texas 79409-1037 USA

800-832-4042

ttup@ttu.edu

Http://www.ttup.ttu.edu

Contents

Foreword   vii

Preface   xi

Acknowledgments   xv

The Barranco Road   1

O'Keeffe and Her Houses   21

Summer Days   43

The Patio   57

A Day with Juan   83

Through the Gate   107

Epilogue: The Wideness and Wonder of the World   117

Notes   131

Appendix A   135

Appendix B   136

Appendix C   140

Appendix D   149

Selected Bibliography   151

Index   155

Foreword

Artists are notoriously circumspect about the origins of their work. It is difficult enough to describe to oneself the mysterious process by which a poem or painting comes into existence, let alone to an apprentice or public audience. How fortunate we are, then, to have John Poling's account of painting with Georgia O'Keeffe. Here is a portrait of an aging artist discovering new ways to create even after she had lost her sight. Painting, she said, "is like the thread that runs through . . . all the other things that make one's life." And for one magical season John Poling helped her to find that thread again.

The outlines of her life are well known. She was born on 15 November 1887 near Sun Prairie, Wisconsin, the second of seven children, and by the eighth grade she had decided to be an artist. She found the right teachers when she needed them: a high school principal who persuaded her to focus on her work; William Merritt Chase, at the Arts Students League in New York City, who encouraged her to "seek to be artistic in every way": in dress, in manners, and in conduct; and Arthur Wesley Dow, at Teacher's College, Columbia University, who convinced her that painting was a matter of "filling space in a beautiful way." This she did for more than sixty years, leaving behind not only one of the most fascinating bodies of work in American art, but also a dynamic example of how to live. "I'm frightened all the time," she once declared. "Scared to death. But I've never let it stop me. Never!"

Her most important mentor was Alfred Stieglitz, the photographer, theorist, and impresario of modern art. "I believe I would rather have

Stieglitz like something—anything I had done—than anyone else I know of," she wrote to a friend in 1916. Not only did he like her work—"Finally, a woman on paper," is what he supposedly remarked when he first saw her drawings—but soon he was her lover and then her husband. He played no small part in turning her into a modern icon, showing and selling her work, photographing her in the nude, working with her in his New York galleries. Theirs was a dynamic creative collaboration, and although they drifted apart long before his death in 1946, he remained her emotional and artistic lodestar.

She moved to northern New Mexico in 1949, having summered in the high desert around Abiquiu for the previous twenty years. It was there, alone, that she completed her late beautiful series of paintings of patio doors and clouds, of bones and roads cut into the sere landscape. Few artists have matched O'Keeffe in so completely marrying their life and work, a fact commented upon by the many people who visited her in Abiquiu, including John Poling, who in the summer of 1975 was a young man at the crossroads of his life. O'Keeffe faced a crisis of her own: unable to work, having lost her vision to macular degeneration, she enlisted Poling to execute a suite of paintings for her.

Their unique collaboration proved fruitful. Poling learned vital lessons from the legendary artist about the creative process, lessons, one imagines, he happily passes on to his students at St. Olaf College, where he teaches philosophy. And the artistic experiment revitalized O'Keeffe, apparently to the dismay of her assistant Juan Hamilton, whose control over her affairs in the last years of her life has been the subject of much controversy and litigation. Unfortunately, the collaboration came to an abrupt end. John Poling did not stay long in O'Keeffe's world, but, as this book reveals, he made the most of an extraordinary opportunity.

The critic Barbara Rose suggests that O'Keeffe's paintings "change[d] the way we see," an idea seconded by Charles Eldredge.

"No less than her paintings," he writes, "her life was a work of art. Like the evening star, hers rose early, and it shined brightest before the dark." *Painting with O'Keeffe* gives us a glimpse of that star shining through the clouds.

Christopher Merrill
College of the Holy Cross

Preface

In the summer of 1976 I began painting with Georgia O'Keeffe. We completed one painting in the Patio Door series that summer, and, the following fall, completed the first two paintings in the *Day with Juan* series. To my knowledge, these are the first and only documented instances of O'Keeffe's collaboration with another person in her career as a painter.

Many of my memories from that time are clear and fresh, reinforced today by journal entries often written the same day. Others are less defined, and, for those, I have reconstructed conversations from remembered words and phrases. This little work makes no claim to completeness; it has no special status. The picture here sets out the shape of my relationship with O'Keeffe over roughly a two-year period, from 1975 to 1977, and gives the reader an idea of what her world was like. For a brief time I was part of that world.

My introduction to O'Keeffe went hand-in-hand with my introduction to northern New Mexico. I moved to Barranco, near the village of Abiquiu, where O'Keeffe lived, late in the summer of 1975. I had two desires: to live in the country and to walk the land. Take away the people, few though they are, and one is left alone with a land whose beauty is almost unbearable.

These pages are written in acknowledgment of a debt to O'Keeffe. A debt to a teacher is an odd thing. If the teacher has taught us well, the learner becomes self-teaching. Hence, the diminishing significance of the teacher and, one would think, the alleviation of the debt. But I return too often to the time with O'Keeffe to feel any lessening in what I owe her. What I have taken is the material for reflection; the task has been to make sense of it, to discern the ways in which that time tutors me.

Undoubtedly she was a teacher of mine, though not only in the trivial sense that she taught me some of the rudiments of oil painting. O'Keeffe was an individual; her world reflected the kind of intention that goes into constituting a self. That range of matters that goes into forming a life is something shown to another, but never said directly. O'Keeffe's life was ordered; things had their place. But everything, from a remark in conversation to the food she ate, was done deliberately.

Perhaps it can be stated like this. The constancy to her passions and pursuits makes for twin accomplishments that limn O'Keeffe's life. One is personal, the other artistic/aesthetic.

Her second, slightly more formal, accomplishment, has to do with her reflections on (her) painting. Throughout her life, in remarks at once spare, dogmatic, and cryptic, O'Keeffe denounced critics who construed her work as mere symbols standing in need of interpretation. She thought such interpretations misunderstood not just her painting but something altogether deeper in the arts. I remember reading to her over several afternoons from a Ph.D. dissertation on the subject of O'Keeffe's paintings; the thesis was that the key to understanding them derived from a kind of psycho-sexual analysis. O'Keeffe thought it was "wrong and nonsense to fill one's head with ideas" having nothing to do with painting.

Drawing, in addition to these clues, on remarks written by her or recorded by others, I think O'Keeffe was not asserting her own way of thinking about art. Instead, she spoke from another understanding of art deemed inadequate by the majority of her critics. Some of these themes are addressed later in the book. Quite rightly, O'Keeffe realized she could not, in a very strong sense of "could," state the meaning of a painting in linguistic form. There was a logical limit on what could be said. The interpretations she contested were, in fact, not interpretations, or even misinterpretations, at all. Her refusal to state the meaning of a painting was indicative of an attitude forced upon her by a grasp of those practices appropriate to an understanding of painting.

What remains most vivid to me is the force of her personality. What is called above a personal accomplishment can be summarized this way. O'Keeffe never described to me as passions her long-standing interests in painting and food preparation and northern New Mexico. Yet the word "passion" captures in another, perhaps more direct form, how her life was organized by her artistic pursuits. Action, reflection on what one is and would like to become, repetition, habit, consistency in wanting, and more, all added up to something, an individual existence well-rooted in patterns of living. A variety of concerns and the activities supporting them had held their place over a period of time: for example, a love of solitude and the Southwest; a preoccupation with health, nutrition, and food preparation; an attention to the arrangement and furnishing of her homes; and, of course, a realization in painting of her own inspirations. To walk into O'Keeffe's world was to walk into a way of life long established.

In this way O'Keeffe is a model, pointing past herself in the sense that her personal achievements transpired, for her as for us, in the realm of wants, needs, deep emotions and passions, interests, talents, responsibilities, and the like. There is no access to that realm without the presence of O'Keeffe. Without the pattern of a life lived according to this range of considerations, her counsel would have been vacuous. Her words would not have hooked up with anything.

In retrospect, O'Keeffe showed me something indirectly, something simple though no less momentous, namely, that each person has the capacity to put his or her life together in a way that stands up to his or her own reflection. O'Keeffe saw life and living as an occasion for all kinds of possibilities. A person could do almost anything, she said. She talked to me as though everything she had accomplished, I could accomplish also.

She did not mean "accomplishments" in terms of wealth or belongings, though she was surrounded by that, too. Nor was she suggesting that being an artist was intrinsically better than other occupations. No, she pointed to something more fundamental, that an enduring satisfaction with what one did could be a reality, and that one's life could bear its own weight. *How* one went about one's life was just as important as, and finally inseparable from, the nature of one's work. But first one had to grow accustomed to the thought that one's deepest needs could become possibilities and, finally, achievements.

O'Keeffe counseled a kind of courageous, go-ahead-and-try attitude. For someone twenty-four years old, somewhat confused about the direction and shape of his own life, her interest was welcome, her presence formidable. Not surprisingly, her example and counsel still ring true.

Acknowledgments

This book has been long in coming to print, and hence owes much to individuals who gave encouragement and assistance over the last ten years.

Donald Sherburne, formerly Professor of Philosophy at Vanderbilt University, made possible a McVean Grant for research on O'Keeffe at Yale's Beinecke Rare Book and Manuscript Library in the summer of 1988. He also worked with me in two courses in aesthetics laying the groundwork for subsequent philosophical work related to O'Keeffe. John Compton and Michael Hodges, also of the philosophy department at Vanderbilt, deserve recognition for constructive conversations on art and painting. My deepest debt is to Paul L. Holmer, formerly Noah Porter Professor of Philosophical Theology at Yale Divinity School, for helping me find an intellectual orientation.

Anonymous readers for Swallow Press and Texas Tech University Press gave me valuable criticisms. Sydelle Kramer, of the Francis Goldin Literary Agency in New York, reviewed the manuscript rigorously in its early stages, for which I thank her.

Some of the events described in the book came about because of the selflessness of certain individuals. James Harrill took an early interest in the story of my collaboration, long before there was any thought of preserving it in words. He introduced me to Hope Aldrich, another figure important in chronicling my collaboration with O'Keeffe. His sudden death in 1997 left unsaid my lasting gratitude for his foresight and for the continued presence in my life of his respect for the truth.

Since 1994 I have taught an interim semester course at St. Olaf College entitled "Georgia O'Keeffe: Philosophy and Art." I thank Edward Langerak, chair of the Philosophy department at St. Olaf, for encouraging me to develop this course, and for making available the very able assistance of Kim Ronning, Dee Bolton, and David Pisa in the preparation of the manuscript. Casaundra Franker edited the manuscript for style and continuity, and the Dean's Fund at St. Olaf contributed financial support for the preparation of the manuscript. The students in the course have stimulated my thinking and furthered my understanding of O'Keeffe in ways I never imagined. To them, and to students in Paracollege and Philosophy department tutorials, especially Shelly Dykema, Megan Allen, Carrie Dirks, and Sara Leland, I am most grateful.

Of the many unexpected and fortuitous associations that resulted from this book, two are especially worthy of mention. While in Denmark during 1989-1990, Christopher Merrill contacted me about contributing to a book on O'Keeffe he was editing. He has continuously supported my work, and it is due to his interest that an excerpt from this book first appeared in print. Jerry Wertheim, of the Santa Fe law firm of Jones, Gallegos, Snead, and Wertheim, provided me with helpful information and contacts over the years.

For the use of Todd Webb's photographs I thank Todd Webb and his representative, Betsy Evans-Hunt. Grateful acknowledgement is also due to Hope Aldrich and the Metropolitan Museum of Art for permission to reproduce relevant materials.

Finally, I note here the immeasurable support given me by my wife, Cindy Jokela. This book would not have happened without her. She, along with my sons, Karlan Johannes, Leslie Eliot, and Noah David, were patient with me when it must have seemed to them that there were far more important things than my working in the study.

I dedicate this book to my father, David Poling, whose belief in this project has never wavered. He was the first to suggest that I write about the time I spent with O'Keeffe. A son could not wish for a better father; a writer could not find a better advocate and agent. His enthusiasm and optimism have never faltered over the years. Those who know him find this unsurprising.

I've been blessed with a father who, in seeking for himself the high ideals of the Christian life, showed his son God's presence in all things.

The Veblen House
January, 1999

To my father

The Barranco Road

The first time I met O'Keeffe I was walking from Barranco to Abiquiu on a dirt road. Some two miles long, it was part of the old road from Santa Fe, through Española, to Abiquiu, before the two-lane blacktop was laid. The old road continued along the Chama River past where the Abiquiu Dam now sits, and eventually crossed the river at a ranch now covered forever by the waters of the dam. One can still follow the road much of the way up-river.

Today, the Barranco road swings off to the south side of U.S. 84, a few hundred feet west of Bode's General Store. It rises up along crumbling white bluffs, then gradually drops down again below the village of Barranco, losing most of the elevation gained before coming to a one-lane wooden bridge over a stream. Cottonwoods grow green and thick between the road and the river. A short hill brings one up to the plateau, where most of the houses are. A small road branches off to the left before the top of this hill; it was there that I rented a two-room adobe home for $50 a month.

It is a fine walk on the Barranco road to Bode's, and I often made the trip to the store for groceries. This particular day was a mid-afternoon in late August, high summer in northern New Mexico. I had not gone far down the road, perhaps a half-mile or so, when a white Mercedes slowed and stopped next to me. My neighbor in Barranco, Mary Grether, was in the driver's seat. During the week Mary worked as O'Keeffe's nighttime companion and cook. She asked if I would like a ride.

I looked past Mary to the passenger seat. A very handsome elderly woman, elegant in appearance and dressed in black, sat next to her, looking straight ahead. When Mary and I spoke the woman's head turned almost imperceptibly in the direction of our voices. Thick gray-white hair was wrapped carefully in long coils on her head. A pin was fastened to her dress below her neck. After I climbed in back, the car moved off slowly, for the Barranco road is notorious for having some of the worst washboards in Rio Arriba County.

Mary introduced me to the woman in front. "John, I don't think you've met Miss O'Keeffe, have you?" O'Keeffe said hello, offering a faint smile.

The trip was short; soon we arrived at Bode's. I remember distinctly a few things from the ride. Mary explained to O'Keeffe who I was and where I lived; she reminded O'Keeffe that my sister and her husband lived in Juan Hamilton's old house. O'Keeffe asked me one or two questions—what I did in Barranco, where I worked, where I had been in New Mexico before moving north. Mostly, I remember eliciting laughter from both of them with a cutting remark or two about the road and the county's inability to maintain it satisfactorily. O'Keeffe turned her head ever so slightly as she listened. Her demeanor was upright and reserved.

At the time, I was completely unfamiliar with O'Keeffe's work and stature, although I had heard her name before.

I moved to Barranco in the summer of 1975 following a lengthy period of discontent and uncertainty. From 1970 until 1973 I attended the College of Wooster in Wooster, Ohio, during which time my family moved from Westchester County in New York to Albuquerque, New Mexico. Two visits to New Mexico during this period reawakened my youthful affection for the land, an affection formed when I was quite young, during family vacations at the Ghost Ranch Conference Center.

The Conference Center (along with the general area around it, usually called "the ranch" for short), is a 22,000-acre conference and retreat facility of the Presbyterian Church (USA), situated fifteen miles north of Abiquiu on U.S. 84. A gift from its former owners, Arthur and Phoebe Pack, to the Presbyterian Church in 1955, the Ranch offered weekly programs in religion, the arts, and the area's stunning nature and geology to families and individuals.

O'Keeffe first came into the Ghost Ranch country—so called because of its old Spanish name, *Rancho de los Brujos,* or Ranch of the Witches—in 1934, and spent the summer at Ghost Ranch. It was from Arthur Pack that O'Keeffe acquired in 1940 the Pack family's former residence, which is located a short distance from the main center of the conference facility.[1]

The restlessness I felt at Wooster, the longing for something undefined, yet seemingly spoken to by the grand openness of New Mexico, precipitated my departure from Wooster to work for a half-year in Albuquerque, and, ultimately, to transfer from Wooster to the University of New Mexico. There I pursued my interest in European history until December of 1975, when I left with two incompletes, which I finished before graduating in 1978.

There followed odd jobs—"odd" in themselves and in relation to the kinds of work I had done previously. For most of the winter and spring of 1975, I worked with a placer gold mining operation in Hillsboro, New Mexico, just south and west of Truth or Consequences. Here, on the great, dry riverbeds east of the Black Mountain Range, an incongruous collection of men dug and washed sand rich in placer gold deposits. I felt somewhat out of place in the company of ranchers, welders, mining engineers, drag-line operators, and the like. Yet, in another way I thrived on the total angularity of the scene, and on the genuine camaraderie of people united by a common pursuit in such an isolated environment. Living in a tiny travel trailer out on the wide plains under a vast sky was often the best compensation of the job.

Since junior high school there had been two constant interests in my life. The first was music, which I pursued as a guitarist in club bands. This presented its own uncertainties as a possible career choice. The end of formal schooling provided an opportunity for me to commit more intently to an avocation to which I had devoted considerable time. But, though I continued playing and performing up to 1983, when I entered Yale Divinity School, I was troubled by what I felt were substantial flaws in the kind of popular, club-oriented music I played. The subject matter of the music and the lifestyle of the musicians were becoming an increasingly poor fit for me. The second interest was in philosophical and theological issues, an interest I kept alive by reading, reflecting, and writing, regardless of my current employment.

Throughout the early 1970s I was unable to clarify for myself the springs of my discontent. The deep affinity I felt with academic pursuits, especially in history, theology, and philosophy, was neutralized by my inability to choose with any conviction the direction my life should take. Self-reflection and examination of my genuine interests failed to provide any resolution of the conflict. The two interests seemed to hang suspended from my emotions, and, in a way, I sought in others, and in a location, what I had to provide myself, and later learned came only from God.

It was against this background that I was compelled by the prospect of moving to northern New Mexico, to the Ghost Ranch country, and living off my savings. Such a move, I thought, would give me time to sort through my thinking, to read and reflect, and to hike a country I longed to know better. While mulling over this prospect, my visits to my sister and her husband who lived in Abiquiu became more frequent. Lesley Poling-Kempes and Jim Kempes, who had met and worked as staff members of the Ghost Ranch, seemed committed to their artistic careers and to living in northern New Mexico. Lesley was a writer and film-maker; Jim a ceramic sculptor, potter, and part-time ceramics teacher at the Ghost Ranch. We hiked together to

A view of the Ghost Ranch country northwest of Abiquiu. Mesa Montosa is the highest point in the ridge line. Photograph by Cindy Jokela.

the rim of, and then up the arroyo into, Cañon del Cobre, and all the while the possibility of living in such country became more and more attractive.

During one of my visits I met Mary Grether, who subsequently introduced me to the village of Barranco, where she lived. Mary rented the old village school house as a residence. Next door to the school was a small adobe she thought might be coming up for rent. From the outside, you could look through a window down the length of the large great room, and I remember vividly how excited I was, the first time I saw it, when I imagined living there. A low doorway led to the kitchen, to which a small bathroom was attached. The long side of the house, opposite the wall across from the school house, faced an overgrown orchard which sloped down to an arroyo, where a stream trickled thinly. Trees, thick and various, surrounded the house. When I turned away from the window and looked up the narrow gated path, past the school house, to the dark rock-green of the high mesas behind, over-hung with summer clouds, black with white edges—at that moment, my heart leaped inside my chest. Within a few weeks I was unloading my furniture, settling into the house, and becoming acquainted with a newly acquired—steady, if uninspiring—'64 Volkswagen Beetle. I was twenty-three years old.

That was a most memorable time, when I was free to walk out the door and disappear into the hills beyond, with no one to know me and no one to follow me. I explored every stream that flowed from the mountains behind my dwelling, sometimes alongside, jumping from stone to stone; sometimes from on high; sometimes sitting under one of the waterfalls. I sat for hours on the hilltops, looking over the valley of the Chama River, and then past it to canyon walls red and yellow in many gradations, to white cliffs, to the ubiquitous green of cedar and piñon, the sky blue and firm overhead. Most days the wind came in short gusts and swirls, blowing up a patch of sand, then subsiding, still heard a step away or seen distantly in the cottonwoods along the river. This world smelled dry but pungent and sweet. All things somehow seemed to fit with each other: the taste watercress from the stream left in one's mouth; the way the scent of a ball of piñon sap pinched one's nostrils; the sound of water dry against the erratic wind; pastel-grained colors juxtaposed with pure ones. Shadows cut darkly into bright sand. The sun was hot, one's skin brown.

Traversing the land brought constant surprises and treasures. I never knew, eyes sweeping the ground, when I might discover an ar-rowhead, or when a potsherd would appear, or when a glance at a rock or wall would reveal old Indian petroglyphs, or when I would stumble upon interesting antlers and bones and skulls. I gathered such treas-ures, and brought them home to mark my new world.

Looking away from the Ghost Ranch toward the Jemez Mountains. The flat-topped mountain on the right is Pedernal. Photograph by Cindy Jokela.

Through late summer and early fall, and as long as I lived in the area, I hiked and re-hiked all the immediate country from Abiquiu to the Ghost Ranch; from Pedernal, the flat-topped mountain dear to O'Keeffe, to Mesa Montosa, which capped the cliffs near her ranch house. Unconsciously, and independently of her world, I began to share with O'Keeffe pleasure in this marvelous countryside.

Before the weather turned too cold, I accompanied my brother-in-law, Jim Kempes, to gather firewood. As was customary among the local inhabitants of that part of New Mexico, our homes were heated primarily, if not solely, by wood stoves. My small adobe had two stoves: a cookstove in the kitchen and a small, oval stove of thin steel in the living/sleeping room.

Where once the water was high, dead wood carried downriver by the Chama River was strewn haphazardly along the hillsides above the Abiquiu Dam. Borrowing a pick-up truck from my parents in Albuquerque and a chain saw from friends in Barranco, we spent a week cutting cottonwood, piñon, and juniper logs to truck-bed size, delivering loads alternately to his house and mine. It was hard work, but the days were clear and bright, and the air, though brisk and edged in coolness, was warm and still, so that the temperature always rose to T-shirt level. It was good to be under the blue sky, to watch the contours of Pedernal unfold and change as the sun arched through the day. Trip after trip we made, and the day's finish was sweet in satisfaction and exhaustion.

As many days were occupied with reading as spent in exploration of my new locale. I began a self-imposed program of reading and note-taking, summarizing books—in history and the philosophy of history, philosophy, theology, and literature—on large filing cards, and writing comments in journals. I hoped my love of reflection and the solitude of my location would make clearer some of the intellectual and emotional preoccupations of the preceding years. I considered during this time the possibility of going to graduate school in history, and wrote to Yale and elsewhere for program bulletins. I never thought at the time that in eight years I would enter Yale Divinity School.

Though I was concerned about future sources of income, there seemed to be some possibilities of employment around the area for me, and, since my needs were insignificant and I was open to any kind of work, provided it left time for my other pursuits, I regarded optimistically the uncertainties of my situation.

My formal introduction into O'Keeffe's world came through Juan (John Bruce) Hamilton, then her combination secretary, business manager, confidant, and companion. Prior to working for O'Keeffe, Hamilton had worked at the Ghost Ranch Conference Center. Hamilton, born in 1946, was six years older than I. He was a graduate of Hastings College in Nebraska, where he earned a studio art degree in 1968; he later studied sculpture at Claremont Graduate School in California for a short period of time. In 1972, Hamilton's father, who was a friend of Jim Hall, the director of the Ghost Ranch Conference Center, offered to help arrange a job for Hamilton in the kitchen at the Ranch.

Once there, Hamilton met O'Keeffe on two occasions in meetings that were uneventful, his presence seemingly unnoticed. On his third visit in 1973, he went to ask her for work, talking to her through a closed screen door. Initially, O'Keeffe said she had none, but as Hamilton walked away she called out to him. "Wait a minute," she said, remembering a project she had. "Do you know how to pack a painting?"[2]

Hamilton had worked for O'Keeffe since the fall of 1973 and traveled with her to Morocco in the winter of 1974. From that point on, Hamilton assisted O'Keeffe with all aspects of her busy life: making appointments for her and taking her to them, helping her in the selection of paintings for her forthcoming book by Viking Press, answering the phone, accompanying her on walks.

In addition, Hamilton spoke fluent Spanish, since he had grown up in South America and Costa Rica, and this gave him a kind of built-in authority with the Spanish-speaking persons who worked for O'Keeffe. During the period from 1974 to 1977, Hamilton supplanted Doris Bry, formerly O'Keeffe's artistic agent for some twenty years, as O'Keeffe's personal representative.

By the time I worked for O'Keeffe, Hamilton was deeply involved in every part of her life, and had assumed duties which included everything from the maintenance of her homes, to the management of her artistic legacy, to meeting whatever day-to-day personal needs she had for companionship and friendship. By the summer of 1976, Hamilton had worked for O'Keeffe for almost three years, during which time she encouraged him to continue in his creative work in ceramic coil pottery. He, too, lived in Barranco, his house high on a plateau connected to the base of the mesas behind the village, a location that overlooked the Chama River valley west of Abiquiu.

I knew of Juan Hamilton from my sister and brother-in-law, Lesley and Jim. Jim came to the Ghost Ranch Conference Center as a conscientious objector during the Vietnam War years, and met Juan there. After living on the ranch for a time, Juan moved to an old adobe home outside of Abiquiu. About the time that Juan purchased what is now his home in Barranco, Jim was ready to move away from the ranch.

Lesley, Jim, and Juan were friends, sharing as they did the common experience of working at the Ghost Ranch and living in northern New Mexico. Once the summer college staff of some thirty students departed from the ranch, there were few persons of similar background left in the area, and the ones that remained often formed natural friendships, even if those friendships were not always close ones.

It was thus that I knew about Juan Hamilton before moving to Barranco, just as I knew about other people who play a role in my story: Mary Grether, who became my neighbor and friend, and Jim Harrill, an accomplished artist who at that time lived in Abiquiu. These people were part of the community of Anglos who formed a compatible subset of the communities of Barranco and Abiquiu, and who intermingled easily and comfortably with the local Hispanic inhabitants.

My links with Juan were various, ranging from distant to more personal ones. Hamilton had been a long-term acquaintance of my family's, both through Les and Jim and through the Ghost Ranch Conference Center, where my family had vacationed in the mid-1960s. I knew of his family through my father's work as a Presbyterian minister, educator, writer and publisher. Ruth and Jim Hall, then the directors of Ghost Ranch, were also close acquaintances of our family

Juan Hamilton (right) with the author at O'Keeffe's Abiquiu house, December 1976. Photographer unidentified. Collection of the author.

as well as of Juan's. When my sister and Jim were married in 1976, Juan participated in all the wedding festivities, from the dinner at Rancho de Chimayo, a well-known restaurant in the little town of Chimayo specializing in New Mexican cuisine, to the wedding ceremony at the Ghost Ranch, to the general socializing of family and friends that preceded the ceremony.

I fit as easily into his world and background as he did into mine. The ground was prepared, as it were, by this web of relations so that by the time I actually met him, it was just a matter of putting a face together with a name already well-known to me. Juan was very much part of the world I was moving into. All that remained was to see how and in what ways we would form a relationship of our own.

I met Juan at Les and Jim's house one evening when he stopped by after his day's work at O'Keeffe's ranch house. Les and Jim were initially my closest and only friends, and we spent many of our days and evenings together. I visited with Juan, Les, and Jim for perhaps an hour that night. When it came time to leave, Juan said I should be sure to stop by his home anytime. His was the last and highest house in the village and, from that vantage point, the view from the front of the house takes in the far red rim of Cañon del Cobre, the white cliffs to the northeast, and the long line of Abiquiu Mesa connecting to the cool, black-green darkness of the mesas behind.

Thereafter, Juan and I got together perhaps once or twice a week for brief times in the evening. He put in long days at O'Keeffe's, and often returned late to his home, having had his evening meal with O'Keeffe. I think his stops at my house allowed him to make a transition from O'Keeffe's world into his own; it also broke for him the routine of home-to-work-to-home. I enjoyed his company, his quick intelligence and sense of humor, and the interest he showed in me.

During our conversations, he found out about my interest in woodworking, and he told me of having worked with house carpenters when he lived on the east coast, and of the appeal remodeling his own home now held for him. We seldom talked about O'Keeffe at any great length. I wanted to know what work he did with her, but not much more than that. It was clear to me, though, in those early conversations, that Juan attached great importance to his relationship with O'Keeffe and the work he was doing for her. He spoke freely of the enormous demands on his time and creative energies that working for her required. I was a sympathetic listener.

Sometimes, Hamilton would come by and ask if I wanted to come up to his house for dinner, or for a beer, and gave me a ride there in his car. On those occasions when I visited his house, I was interested to see what books he had, what kind of coil pots he had made, the O'Keeffe prints he had hanging on his walls.

Juan furnished his house tastefully and sparely; a few chairs where needed, bed and stereo, a round kitchen table, and so on. The colors were white or off-white, accented by the natural, exposed wood ceilings and floor-boards. It was a large house for one person, and those parts under construction created a feeling of disarray that contrasted with the other parts of the house. He was rebuilding most of his house, adding a large back room and a second floor.

Oftentimes our conversation was about the work he envisaged, and I was eager to hear him describe how one went about doing basic kinds of carpentry tasks, or working with adobe and mud plaster. We chatted easily as he walked me through his house, sketching in the air his remodeling ideas. On other evenings, he showed me slides of where he had lived in Vermont before moving to the Southwest. Over all, I felt in coming to know Juan that I was gaining a friend, and I looked forward to the times we spent together as one of the unexpected benefits of living in Barranco.

During one of my visits, Hamilton asked me whether I would like to work for him on his house along with a friend of his, Ted, who was helping him with it. I worked for Hamilton in one- or two-week stretches much of that fall. The employment periods fell into chunks of time for a variety of reasons: sometimes Hamilton could not be there, or Ted was gone, or supplies did not arrive, or the next step in building was unclear, or I wanted to go hiking. The tasks I had to perform were varied. With a draw knife I peeled bark from pine trees felled in the forest by Hamilton and Ted to make vigas, the long, round, exposed beams used in traditional adobe houses to support the ceiling boards and roof. I mixed mud for adobes and helped lay adobe bricks. The days were perfect, with week after week of blue sky and sun. Far below, along the Chama River, the cottonwoods gradually changed to yellow. I was grateful to Hamilton for the work; when I thanked him, I remember his marked surprise, as though I had referred to something irrelevant.

During this fall period I discovered many of the complexities of Hamilton's personality. We shared general interests, living, as we did in the Abiquiu and Ghost Ranch area, somewhat outside the mainstream American culture. We had had similar college experiences and connections with the Presbyterian church: his father had worked for the church in South America and New York; mine had been a pastor, publisher, and writer. Juan was also knowledgeable about building and carpentry, something I wanted to learn more about. He could be thoughtful in occasional, spontaneous actions, such as offering to take my brother-in-law Jim and me out to eat at the Rancho de Chimayo restaurant, or when he suddenly and unexpectedly gave me an old South American blanket.

These genuinely attractive features of his personality were hedged in by others that were less so. For instance: Ted and I worked mostly alone, but Juan would join us for at least a brief period each day to oversee our work. One time he joined Ted in laying adobes while I mixed mortar in a large pit. I shoveled mortar into a wheelbarrow and took to it to them. Juan paused in his work. "Four years of college and this is all you can do," he said, laughing, but with sarcasm in his voice.

On another occasion, when he stopped by to watch us work, he criticized how we laid adobes, or how we peeled vigas, for example, simple activities which, when he demonstrated them, were executed exactly as we had. "What a life working up here: a great location, getting paid good money while I'm working hard for O'Keeffe." His idea of good money was the minimum wage I earned: $2.50 an hour.

When he originally asked me to work for him, I made sure it was acceptable to him that some weeks I would work less than a full week, or not at all. But eventually that became a source of resentment also. "You've got it made, working when you want," he said several times and in various ways. It became impossible for Ted and me to predict what Hamilton's mood would be when he finally appeared on the scene.

At first, I didn't take Juan's remarks too personally. In part, I felt he wanted to be working with us, on his house. I also saw that he was a perfectionist. But then again, so was I: I strove to do well and correctly whatever I undertook. I always asked for his advice or direction. After a while, I could tell the difference between legitimate instruction or correction and personal put-down, and, increasingly, the latter dominated.

Later, when I had occasion to reconsider this time, it seemed to me as though some of the best characteristics of his personality—his humor and thoughtfulness, for example—began to atrophy through disuse. Not every encounter was unfortunate, but the occasions were frequent enough. Transpiring as they did against a background of human expectation and intercourse in an isolated part of New Mexico, where there were fewer person-to-person contacts to begin with, they stood out in greater relief.

The fall passed quickly. The air turned colder, and one's eye shifted from the leafy brilliance of the cottonwoods to the muted gray of their trunks and bare branches. Piñon smoke from wood stoves now scented the air on my walk home from work. Most of the construction at Hamilton's place came to a halt. It was then that he told me someone was needed to house-sit O'Keeffe's Abiquiu home while she stayed at her ranch house, and wondered whether I would be interested. The Abiquiu house was located off the plaza of the small town of Abiquiu, overlooking U.S. 84 going east-southeast toward Española. This same road in the opposite direction leads to the Ghost Ranch Conference Center, where O'Keeffe's other house—referred to by those in her household as "the ranch house" or "the ranch"—was situated in a more remote setting. The distance between the two was around twenty minutes.

The job seemed like a perfect way to supplement the money I had saved, and I agreed to do it.

One afternoon in the spring of 1976, I met Hamilton while driving to Bode's. He rolled down his window and we spoke car-to-car. He mentioned something to the effect that O'Keeffe wanted the trim on her Ghost Ranch house painted. Would I be interested? I said I was. The following afternoon he came to my house. The Ghost Ranch job, he estimated, would last over the summer. In addition, he had some projects to be done at his home. He also asked whether I would house-sit for him. He thought he would spend most of the summer—July, August, and part of September—in New York, overseeing the printing of color plates of O'Keeffe's paintings for a new book from Viking Press.

Hamilton said he would pay me five dollars a night to look after his house and garden, and that O'Keeffe could afford to pay me $3.75 to $4.00 an hour, which seemed like good money at the time. He reminded me there were only two "factories" in Abiquiu: one was O'Keeffe and the other was the Ghost Ranch Conference Center. Later in the summer, his friend Ted would be staying at Hamilton's home again, so I would not be completely tied to the house. Before he left for New York, Juan said, he would take me to the Ghost Ranch house, so I could get an idea of the extent of the project, and he ended by saying I could start by working around the Abiquiu house, as well as up at his.

I was nervous my first day at the Abiquiu house. The location and grounds are impressive. The house sits on a small plateau at the edge of town, overlooking the winding highway that curves east toward Española. Like many adobe homes, even the largest, the house's mass is softened by rounded corners and one-story roof lines, as well as by the deep browns and earth tones of the building material, which draw the walls into the shapes and colors of the surrounding hills and sand slides.

I did not know what was expected of me nor what kind of work I was to do. Often in the morning, as it turned out, the staff gathered in an open area between the wing of the house where O'Keeffe's room and studio were, and the main part of the house, which was detached from the studio. At that time, Hamilton, sometimes with O'Keeffe watching inside the sliding screen door of the studio area, talked to the staff, telling them what to do, and pointing out what special tasks needed attention. There were four of us there that first morning: Candelaria or "Candy" Lopez, who was the day-cook and house-keeper; Esteban Suazo, or "old Steven" as I called him, Candy's father, who did most of the grounds work; a young man of high school age, perhaps one of Candy's sons; and me. Hamilton told me there was some pruning of branches that Steven needed help with, so my first day was spent outside on the grounds, clearing and collecting brush. I worked for several weeks in Abiquiu: on the grounds, moving boxes, fixing screen doors, and the like.

One cloudy afternoon Hamilton and I drove to the ranch house, where O'Keeffe would spend most of the summer. The trim on the house was in terrible shape. Some of the wooden trim around the large picture windows was cracked or rotting and needed replacement; many of the other windows could not be opened at all due to similar problems. All needed attention. As we walked around the house, Hamilton pulled off large chunks of dried putty from around the windows. The enormous door on the garage also needed work. He pointed out minor repairs—replacing rotting wood and trim on doors or above windows, for example—to be made before painting. He said I could expect O'Keeffe to ask me to help her with various other chores, and that I was to drop whatever I was doing to assist her.

For several weeks prior to Hamilton's eastern sojourn my work was divided between his house and O'Keeffe's—a not unwelcome situa-tion, if an awkward one, since the person responsible for hiring me wanted as much work as possible done at both places. I was asked to build a large shipping crate for some of O'Keeffe's paintings, to be sent later by air freight from Albuquerque. The upstairs of Hamilton's house was unfinished, and his tools and table-saw were there in a makeshift work area. The large square frame I built from one-by-six lumber was fitted with plywood front and back, with only the latter attached.

Once at the studio in Abiquiu, O'Keeffe and I watched Hamilton as he placed several paintings, carefully wrapped and protected, in the crate. Both of them then watched me as I added extra padding before securing the top. Throughout the process O'Keeffe contributed a string of remarks, mostly concerns and reminders to be careful, while Hamilton and I worked together. More than once Hamilton responded playfully to O'Keeffe, chiding her with good humor and telling her to relax, catching my eye while feigning to roll his. Still she continued.

"Georgia, if you can't be quiet, I'm going to put you in there with your paintings," he said, looking at me.

O'Keeffe abruptly became quiet, both hands resting on her cane, a slight "humph" preceding her silence. No sooner had she quieted, when she started again with a by now quite familiar: "You must be sure to . . ."

"All right," Hamilton said, popping up, putting his arms around O'Keeffe's arms and under her legs, and lifting her. O'Keeffe protested—"Juan, *Juan*, now stop it! Oh my, put me down"—and laughed, as did I, while Hamilton wrested from her a guarantee that she would be quiet.

I remember the morning Hamilton left. He and I were to drive in O'Keeffe's Mercedes to Albuquerque, where I would drop him off at the airport. The morning was clear, cool, and bright when I arrived in Abiquiu. Mary was still there; she usually left at 8:30 or so, but today was different. O'Keeffe had eaten breakfast. Hamilton was going to eat, but there seemed to be endless details requiring his attention before he could sit down to breakfast. The house was abustle with people running here and there; some of the day help coming in; Mary trying to gauge when to cook Hamilton's breakfast; others, such as me, hovering, looking for a chance to be useful. All I could do was watch. Hamilton finally sat down to eat a breakfast of scrambled eggs and garlic just prepared by Mary. He took several bites, and then, for no perceptible reason, suddenly lashed out cruelly at Mary, who, as dumbfounded as I, left, upset and shattered. His transition from one mood to another was startling. We finally left by mid-morning, with Hamilton driving the two-hour trip to Albuquerque. He talked most of the time, about himself and his goals, about the book project, about what O'Keeffe was like, and about what jobs he wanted done. An air of self-importance suffused everything he said.

I looked forward to the return drive alone. Along the east side of the interstate there is still evidence of the old dirt road north from Albuquerque to Santa Fe, a road no doubt familiar to O'Keeffe from her early days in New Mexico. At one point there is a deep cut through a long, flat hill, west of the Sandia Mountains and north of Albuquerque, where the old road is clearly visible.

As one leaves Albuquerque, foothills and plains wend their way westward and down to the Rio Grande river, delineated along either shore by the bosque, a wide area dense with cottonwoods that hold the river like two shimmering bands, green or gold or gray depending on the season. Continuing northward, the Sandias recede as a large mass of mesa and mountain, the Jemez Mountains, gradually assumes prominence to the west. The highway climbs the steep La Bajada hill to a high plateau. Looking back now toward Albuquerque, to the south and west, one can see faintly undulating plains and mountains, many with mesas extending like the fingers of a hand. To the north, the mountains around Santa Fe, the Sangre de Cristo Mountains, are suddenly visible as one rounds a bend and begins to descend from the plateau. Santa Fe is another fifteen minutes or so away; Abiquiu well over an hour.

O'Keeffe and Her Houses

In an odd way, I became acquainted with O'Keeffe when I house-sat for her in Abiquiu, long before circumstances brought us together, person to person. Being in her house alone defined my first impressions of her. I saw the obvious financial accomplishment that made possible the general maintenance and furnishing of such an estate.[1]

It was difficult to take in all at once the entirety of the compound, with patio, garden, library, detached studio with O'Keeffe's bedroom, living, dining, and storage rooms, and on and on, not to mention the variety and kind of furnishings and the personnel necessary for maintaining two homes and keeping up the lifestyle of their owner. The guest room where I slept and the large adjoining bathroom nearly equaled the size of my two-room adobe in Barranco. It was not without some shock that I returned home after these first encounters with the Abiquiu home.

Everywhere in O'Keeffe's house was the impress of an aesthetic refinement. The guest room was furnished simply: a plain white bedspread, a small table and chair, a nightstand with a phone next to the bed. Long, thin splints of piñon, slivers almost, were stacked vertically in the quarter-round corner fireplace. In the dining room, wooden captain chairs surrounded an ample table of plain wood. The rooms were neither too empty nor overfilled with furnishings.

I clearly sensed the governing intent implicit in what I saw, much as one gathers on first hearing the complexity of a musical composition without discerning its component and interwoven parts, or feels, in reading a great writer, that more was said than actually written. I felt surrounded by an intention easy to recognize after an initial unfamiliarity. My first understanding of O'Keeffe's aesthetic sensibilities ("aesthetic," because they were not limited to her art alone) came not through her paintings themselves, but through the powerful orchestration evident in her Abiquiu home.

Had these possessions been arranged with an eye less capable and refined, the variety of objects alone would overwhelm even the largest room. Yet O'Keeffe so ordered the elements of her world that each was highlighted while still congruous with the whole. To walk through the Abiquiu home made one feel the space was utilized with propriety. Both object and observer were given due consideration. Elegance and economy melded in a single gesture. The evenness and proportion throughout her two homes testified to O'Keeffe's breadth and concentration.

The ascetic overtones were unmistakable; simplicity, not barrenness, ruled, and this made richer the visual pleasures of her homes. It was irrelevant whether the actual things of my world were the same as O'Keeffe's because of the way in which hers were arranged and presented. There was never a trace of the arbitrary or the forced. O'Keeffe once wrote that someone had sent her seashells, that they were lovely and hearkened back to a time earlier in her life, but that they fit another world, not the Southwest.

Most times of the year, and particularly during the summer, O'Keeffe preferred the ranch house. It was smaller and more remote, shaped like a squared-off letter U, with the open part facing Pedernal far in the distance. Tall, sandstone cliffs stood some distance from the back side of the house.

There was a center patio surrounded on three sides by the wings of the house. Doors opened onto the patio from different rooms—guest rooms, bedrooms, studio and kitchen. A covered area six feet in width fit the inside of the U, and allowed one to walk under cover anywhere around the patio. One or two old Pueblo-style wooden ladders with rounded, grayish rungs led to the roof. O'Keeffe told me she used to climb up there and sleep on summer nights when the weather was good.

On the patio, sagebrush bushes had been left to grow large among flat slabs of stone. Their smell punctuated the air sharply. In early morning the dry air, cool and moistened by a light dew, was scented with sage and sand. The thick fragrance of sage, and occasional whiffs from split piñon and cedar firewood stacked under the overhang, mingled in the air off the land surrounding the house. One's nostrils nearly smarted.

The ranch house was nearer one of two "Chimney Rocks," tall, weather-chiseled sandstone columns. O'Keeffe walked regularly to the cliffs, separated by erosion from the closest Chimney Rock. One could vary one's approach to the cliffs, either by walking on a relatively flat but gently rising plain to the cliff base, or by following a route over some of the small foothills, with ups and downs sometimes steep and abrupt, sometimes evenly modulated.

The earth in places is a dark, brownish red. Gently cracked, the texture of the ground underfoot is rough where small stones, rocks, and pieces of caked earth stand high on the hardened surface. Pastel shades of sand, rich in overtones, ease here and there one into the other: peach into red; purple and light lavender into chalky gray, then further to a burnt yellow-orange. One can sit below or between the two Chimney Rocks and watch thick clouds move slowly over nearby mesas before disappearing over the cliffs.

The clarity of vision is breathtaking. The dry air, the abundance of direct and ambient light, permeate everything in one's field of vision. Features of every kind in this world are thrown into clear relief, a relief tempered as the day passes by trembling, transparent waves of heat that

Red hills rise from the plain near O'Keeffe's ranch house. One of the two Chimney Rocks is visible in the upper left; the highest formation is Mesa Montosa. O'Keeffe's house was some distance to the left of Chimney Rock. Photograph by Cindy Jokela.

visibly shimmer, like flame-fingered extensions rising from the tops of the light desert grasses. The heat makes a motionless flat plain tingle with movement, animating otherwise still trees and grasses and distant hills.

The cliffs behind the ranch house are washed gray from the crumbling surface on top, the long rim line broken where rock has tumbled below, leaving one or two slightly curved cuts, which act like broken windows to the clouds disappearing in back. The hills at the base are streaked with white, off-red, gray, and piñon green. O'Keeffe claimed she found every color she wanted by looking out her window.

Red hills and sandstone cliffs behind O'Keeffe's ranch house. O'Keeffe loved to walk in the area and often made it the subject of her paintings. Photograph by Cindy Jokela.

When I worked for O'Keeffe, a studio occupied the center portion of the ranch house, connecting the two longer sides. A fireplace with a large deer skull with antlers hanging above it faced the entrance of the studio, slightly off center to the right. The room was painted white, with plain wooden doors and floors. On either side of the fireplace, tall, wide windows faced the sandstone cliffs.

O'Keeffe said the light in this room was ideal for painting. Though the windows in the room faced north, away from direct sunlight as the day progressed, the massive cliffs reflected ample indirect light, its intensity diffused by the predominantly gray tone of the cliff walls. O'Keeffe was right about the lighting; when we began to paint, it was

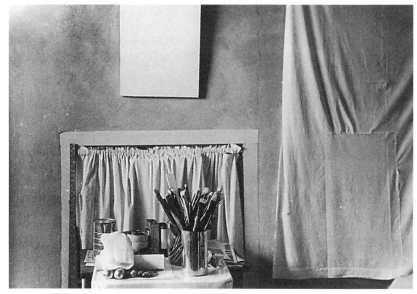

O'Keeffe's studio at her Ghost Ranch home. The worktable with painting equipment was to the right as one entered the studio. Sandstone cliffs and Mesa Montosa were visible through the tall windows of the studio. Photograph © Todd Webb (b. 1905), Untitled, nd, gelatin silver photograph, Todd Webb Study Collection, Museum of Fine Arts, Museum of New Mexico, Gift of Mr. and Mrs. Todd Webb.

only by the end of the day that it became difficult to see, so that we were forced to turn on one of the overhead fluorescent lights. When we painted, the canvas always faced the windows or was angled slightly to one side.

To the right of the fireplace stood one or two large easels. Though heavy and well-made, they were wobbly from years of use. They could be adjusted to accept all but the very largest canvas. Built into the wall on the south side of the studio was a storage area, a small closet with shelves holding paint brushes, small boxes of paint and strips of sample colors, and other painting accessories. O'Keeffe's bedroom was in the north corner, to the far left as one entered the studio, away from the door and somewhat separated from the studio by a partial dividing wall and another room. This granted her some privacy while permitting her staff to come and go through the studio.

Unfortunately, the earth underneath this house, as well as under the nearby house of Ghost Ranch Conference Center director Jim Hall, was unstable. (O'Keeffe claimed there used to be an underground river there.) The plaster walls were forever cracking as the house settled and re-settled over the years, and had to be regularly repaired. Ida Archuleta, one of the day-cooks, was also a skilled adobe plasterer. Among the more traditional Hispanic people in New Mexico, the women did the actual mud plastering, while a man—in Ida's case, one of her sons—mixed a plaster of mica, sand, mud, and water for the plasterers to apply.

O'Keeffe esteemed Ida's skill. She asked me whether I had ever seen adobe plastering done, and insisted on bringing me outside one day when Ida was plastering a wall. Ida used a small sponge to smooth the ribs left in the fresh plaster by her hands. Even shadowed by the portal, the mica glistened in the wet coat. Ida worked slowly and steadily. Days later, after the walls dried, I could still see broad, gently raised arcs where she plastered. Her work was visible inside in the dining room near the kitchen, where a large crack on the wall by the fireplace had been filled and replastered. There the micaceous plaster was burnt red-brown, like the tones sometimes seen in primitive clay pots.

I became familiar with the home in Abiquiu through house-sitting. This was the first "work" I did for O'Keeffe. I arrived at 5 P.M. when old Steven left, and departed in the morning when Candy and Steven arrived. The guest room I slept in was quite large, and formed one of the walls to the left upon entering the inner grounds through a wire-mesh gate. A bathroom with an enormous, deep bathtub was attached to the guest room. I was free to explore and use the main part of the house, but not O'Keeffe's studio and bedroom wing. Some of O'Keeffe's paintings hung on the walls. One from the Patio Door series was in the living room, while a *Black Rock* painting hung in the dining room.

The living room was an impressive room. Bancos (adobe benches built into the wall and covered with plaster) ran along the right wall. Encased under a piece of glass somewhat recessed from the level of the banco was a beautiful rattlesnake skeleton set on sand, the delicate bones carefully displayed. Small, smooth rocks were grouped along the banco; pillows lined the wall. At the far end of the room, drapes covered a wall of windows.

Adjacent to the dining and living rooms, and open in warm weather to the rest of the house, was a modest courtyard surfaced in pebbles. O'Keeffe's enormous jade plants were placed there in the summer, where they received water when it rained, and sunlight during various parts of the day. A piece of gray cedar, weathered and sinuous, rested in the corner. On the opposite side of the kitchen a door opened to a dark, cool room O'Keeffe called the Indian room. Several steps descended to floor level. Some large Indian pots lined the wall, and a rug or two lay on the floor.

Two other rooms merit description. One was an enormous storage room where O'Keeffe kept her paintings. I was here with O'Keeffe on several occasions when she wanted to locate a particular painting. Like phonograph records in a rack, the paintings were stacked in two levels, side by side. During a visit by Barbara Rose (an art critic who later appeared in Perry Miller Adato's film on Georgia O'Keeffe) the three of us spent part of a morning in that room. O'Keeffe and Rose sat in chairs while I pulled out a number of paintings for them. For me the occasion was a glimpse into an unfamiliar world.

There was another room next to this, a combination storeroom and work area, with a flat table or work surface in the center. Along the right wall and the back of the room were shelves where, among other things, copies of posters and Christmas cards were kept. Once, in Abiquiu, after a morning break, O'Keeffe unexpectedly said she had something she wanted to give me, and had me get a key. I followed her outside to the patio, where the black door stood locked, and opened it. She went to a shelf along the wall, and then directed me to some old Christmas cards, saying simply, "You should have one of these." The card was a reproduction of *Starlight Night* (No. 12 in *Georgia O'Keeffe*).

The Abiquiu house was an enormous adobe, its rooms and wings connected in odd and unpredictable ways. O'Keeffe's bedroom overlooked the road to Española, El Rito Mountain, and the mesas stretching north toward Taos. Directly to the east stood the brooding presence of Abiquiu Mesa.

Every Monday most of the Abiquiu irrigation ditch was diverted to water O'Keeffe's grounds, a notable fact given the role of water in the area. The ditch carried fresh spring water flowing out of the mesas behind Abiquiu; Barranco has a similar water supply. Several springs join together to provide Abiquiu's drinking and irrigation water. Drinking water is stored in a tank and piped into the houses, except for those that have their own wells. There was enough water for the weekly watering of gardens and small fields, the process accomplished by means of an intricate system of irrigation ditches fed directly by the springs.

Springs sustain life in this country. They are crucial for growing anything in northern New Mexico, where rainfall is unpredictable, the soil poor, and the earth baked hard by the sun. Each village landowner with water rights gets water from the ditch every week for a prescribed part of a day. Sometimes several people use the water at once, each taking a small portion. The goal is to give the ground a good, long soaking, in the hope that the water will hold whatever crops are planted for another week, and perhaps even be supplemented by a shower or two. It behooves landowners to utilize their water rights regularly, as they can be lost from lack of use.

Almost all of O'Keeffe's vegetables were grown in her garden in Abiquiu, minded in the summer by her sister Claudia, assisted by her Cuban maid, who always came with her. They tended it themselves, or directed old Steven in various tasks while O'Keeffe lived at the ranch. The garden was quite substantial; it covered an enormous area inside the large adobe walls surrounding the better part of O'Keeffe's compound.

O'Keeffe's meals were well-balanced, prepared from fresh ingredients, and supplemented by a battery of vitamin pills. She had carefully investigated the role of a balanced diet in maintaining good health, using a variety of the kind of cookbooks that, today, we would call "health" books—another instance of the care and attention O'Keeffe brought to daily living. Breakfast was small, lunch was the main meal of the day, and dinner often consisted of hot or cold soup accompanied by a hearty homemade bread. Sometimes beer was served with lunch. O'Keeffe kept on hand small, seven-ounce cans of Coors beer, which was just the right amount, she claimed, for a midday meal. If there were guests for lunch, a special dish was prepared.

Once a week I drove to Santa Fe to purchase specific items at the health food store on Galisteo and the butcher on Cerrillos Road. From the butcher I bought several pounds of top round of beef, which was to be ground three times. Back at O'Keeffe's this was prepared like a meat loaf, delicately seasoned with chives, and usually accompanied by strips of green chile chilled on a plate, sprinkled with crushed garlic, and covered with a thin layer of olive oil. Mary had told me about O'Keeffe's love of garlic, and said that, on occasion, they ate garlic cloves whole while Mary prepared the evening meal.

Sometimes O'Keeffe's peculiarities must have seemed an onerous burden for her staff. She wanted things done in a certain fashion, and, if her mood was off that day, minor deviations could elicit an irritable response from her and make for tense relations all around. For the most part everyone knew what O'Keeffe expected, and they had long since grown accustomed to keeping things the way she wished.

One morning, in the middle of summer, O'Keeffe was in Abiquiu. Mary was still there when I arrived, getting O'Keeffe's things ready to take to the ranch. I was to transport cumbersome or extra items, since O'Keeffe and Mary were making the trip with the two chow dogs, Jingo and Inca. I had been loading boxes of food items into O'Keeffe's small Audi station wagon, and, on my second trip from the kitchen, I overheard a commotion in the large walk-in pantry, where flour, spices, pots and pans, and other kitchen implements were kept. O'Keeffe, seemingly upset, was talking to Steven and Candy. When I asked Mary what had happened, she smiled cautiously: O'Keeffe thought some flour was missing and she was convinced one of the staff members had taken it. Mary and I both smiled at the absurdity of the scene. When I returned, I hovered by the pantry, watching the exchange between this elderly woman and her helpers of many years. At one point I caught O'Keeffe's eye. Almost imperceptibly, unobserved by anyone else, her stern expression momentarily relaxed. I told her I would drive ahead to open the ranch house.

An hour later she and Mary arrived. As we were unloading the Mercedes, I made a remark to the effect that "Mrs. O'Keeffe" had all of us trembling back there, using "Mrs." instead of "Miss" to chide her gently about her stern manner. "I'd hate to think what it would be like to be on your *bad* side," I ventured. There was a short pause before she let go and laughed at herself. Then we all laughed together at the picture of O'Keeffe taking to task her dumbfounded workers.

Prior to Hamilton's departure for New York, O'Keeffe, who had been staying at the ranch house, returned to Abiquiu, where more of the things associated with the business side of her life were located.

However, no sooner had Hamilton left than O'Keeffe relocated to the ranch house. This was always an event since a number of articles, from clothes and food to mail and dogs, had to be shifted from one place to the other. The day O'Keeffe moved, Mary asked me to come into Abiquiu and drive O'Keeffe's station wagon to the ranch. She and O'Keeffe would drive out at the same time—accompanied, of course, by the chows, who traveled with O'Keeffe. The four of them made an unusual sight: the two dogs, one black, one cinnamon-colored, sitting in the back seat; O'Keeffe and Mary in front, both wearing sunglasses; the whole entourage in a white Mercedes.

That day I did little work on the ranch house. Instead, I unloaded cars, opened doors and windows, moved boxes and furniture, and helped O'Keeffe and Mary settle in.

I started my work at the ranch house several days before Hamilton left, preparing for a primer coat of paint by scraping, replacing putty, and generally repairing the trim where necessary. On a typical work day, I arrived at the ranch by 8:30. The drive from Barranco takes around twenty minutes. The road winds as it climbs a steep hill out of the Chama River valley below Barranco and Abiquiu, before dropping abruptly to the flats that extend for many miles as one heads north to the ranch. The dominant presence crossing the flats is the large, flat-topped mountain called Pedernal, which has appeared in many of O'Keeffe's works. Pedernal sits on the other side of the Chama River overlooking a small town called Cañones. Today the river is dammed not far from Abiquiu, and is fast becoming a recreational eyesore. The large "lake" created by the dam is visible for much of the remainder of the drive.

By the time I arrived, O'Keeffe had usually been up for several hours. She woke early, at 5 A.M. or so, and rose soon after. She did not always sleep well, and kept a record player by her bed, so she could listen to recorded books during the night. Sometimes, when I arrived, I found her sitting at the table in the kitchen, looking out the window, her head turned away from the door. She sat on a padded banco at the table where we ate our meals. Two large picture windows offered a view of the sandstone cliffs to the north and east.

O'Keeffe began to lose her central vision in 1971 at the age of eighty-four. The degeneration she experienced in her retina entailed the loss of her acute vision, though she retained some measure of peripheral vision. When I was first around her I was unaware of her loss of vision or of how extensive that loss was. The problem was impossible to discern, given my brief glimpses of her, and subsequently I realized how living in two homes where everything stayed physically the same made it seem to the casual observer as if she saw better than she did. Her knowledge of where everything was or should be, coupled with what little remained of her vision, misled many a person less familiar with her than I was.

One morning I was working on the east side of the house. My shirt was off; it was still cool and comfortable. I was standing on a ladder by one of the kitchen windows when Mary came out the side entrance. She said Miss O'Keeffe wondered whether I could help her with something.

I put my shirt on and followed Mary through the kitchen across the patio to O'Keeffe's studio. O'Keeffe stood just inside the door, dressed in a plain, white cotton dress. She looked as cool as the morning. Her demeanor was calm and steady, always distinguished, a faint smile across her lips. She and Mary had been cleaning out a small storage closet and had some boxes to be moved and rearranged. The task took only a moment.

As the week went by I was repeatedly asked to help her with a variety of small chores. Sometimes it was too dark in a closet, and she wanted me to find something. On another occasion, after lunch and a rest she took immediately afterwards, she asked me to read to her from a Ph.D. thesis on her art. Mary had read some to her in the evenings. I began where she had stopped.

It was dreadful material, very dry, overworked, and unimaginative. I did not know what to make of it at the time. The writer took a psycho-sexual approach: O'Keeffe's paintings were all symbols of this or that "hidden" feature of her personality, and invariably concealed a sexual secret. O'Keeffe often interrupted my reading, asking me to explain a word or phrase, or, surprisingly to me, to ask what I thought about what was being said.

"It must be nice to find out what you've been doing all these years," I remarked.

O'Keeffe was pleased with the tone of my comment. When I asked her what she thought, I already had an idea of what her response would be, for, as I read, she would shake her head or interrupt me at some particularly far-fetched remark. She said she never cared for such interpretations of her work. The subject matter of her painting was, quite simply, the beautiful and colorful shapes that she saw. She wanted to paint them, and that was all there was to it.

I was startled to hear this. "There must be more to it than that," I thought. According to what little education I had in such matters, a piece of art, as the dissertation writer suggested, expressed a feature of the artist's personality, or was, perhaps, a reflection of a hidden or unconscious aspect of that personality. In unequivocal terms, O'Keeffe spoke out simply, dogmatically against such a view.

Later that afternoon, while I read out loud, O'Keeffe dozed off. She rested in a thickly padded easy chair covered with white cotton. Her eyes had been closed for some time, but I watched now as her head shifted to one side. I paused in my reading, then stopped.

The room was quiet. A hot afternoon breeze swished around the sagebrush bushes just outside, sometimes coming through the screen door. The studio was cool and dark; the summer day blazed several steps away. The world was still but for the sound of the wind.

We sat like that for ten minutes or so. Then O'Keeffe quietly roused herself.

She asked me where we had been, and said I should start reading again. I read for a while longer before she tired of the material.

"I guess I've heard enough of that." She looked at me. "Do you have work to do?" She knew I did, and I answered affirmatively. "You'd better go do that. Can you read for me tomorrow?" I said I could.

A half hour remained before I left for home.

A day later Mary again came outside where I was working, this time earlier in the morning, just before she was to leave around half past eight or nine o'clock. She and O'Keeffe had not finished going through the mail. O'Keeffe wondered whether I could read it to her.

I found O'Keeffe in the studio, sitting on the same easy chair among other chairs placed in a semi-circle before the fireplace. She was dressed in white, the ever-present pin with the initials "OK" near her throat. (The pin, a brass piece about 1½ by 4 inches forming her initials, had been given to her by the sculptor Alexander Calder.) A stack of letters was next to her.

"Do you think you can read these to me?" I was struck by the oddness of her request, considering I was in her employment.

I said English had never been too difficult for me, and I took the letters.

I had quickly discovered O'Keeffe's predilection for humor employing irony and sarcasm, which emphasized the absurdities in people and circumstances while making light of them. I was careful not to overindulge in this, and injected it sparingly into our conversation and banter. But as our days passed together it became a great pleasure to make her laugh. Her smile was handsome, and laughter accentuated the warmth and graciousness of her personality. She liked my verbal caricatures, and her acceptance went far toward helping me gain confidence in her presence, and toward making us comfortable with each other.

O'Keeffe reads her correspondence while seated in the wide portal surrounding the interior of the ranch house. The photo was probably taken in the 1960s before she lost most of her eyesight. Her studio is on the right. Photograph © Todd Webb (b. 1905), Untitled (O'Keeffe Reading a Letter), nd, gelatin silver photograph, Todd Webb Study Collection, Museum of Fine Arts, Museum of New Mexico, Gift of Mr. and Mrs. Todd Webb.

Her correspondence, as could be expected, covered both personal and business matters. Often there was a note from an admirer. The business concerns I set aside for Hamilton. Helping her with the correspondence entailed not only reading letters to her, but answering them, too. She said there was paper on the table by the picture window, and a pen for jotting down her answers. Her replies were economical and to the point, the sentences formed in her characteristic fashion, though they seemed terribly long to me as I attempted to take down every word. For my own peace of mind I reread her replies to her, which, as often as not, she changed slightly. One letter I answered was a series of questions from Perry Miller Adato, who was gathering additional material for her documentary on O'Keeffe.

When we finished the stack she said: "Well, I don't see why you can't go ahead and type them up. Can you type?" I said I could. "Juan will be gone for some time, and we can't have Mary do them all. I'm going to rest. I think this would be a good time to do these, don't you?" She stood up carefully, moving toward the patio door. We walked over to the east wing of the house, through the kitchen and dining room to a back guest room. There was a table with a typewriter and stationery. She said to bring the letters to her to sign when they were done.

I opened the drapes away from the sunny side of the house. Over the bed was one of her paintings of a cottonwood tree, a blend of greens and glowing yellows where shapes often diffused into swaths of color. I sat for a long moment, happy to be doing her correspondence, entrusted with what I thought an important responsibility.

After typing I returned to the studio. I sat until she rose from her rest, which was not long after I arrived. I learned to announce my presence if I thought she was awake and unaware of it, for I startled her on several occasions by simply walking up to her unannounced. She did not always hear footsteps in the room.

I read the replies to her. On one or two she wanted to add another line or change the contents entirely. Those I retyped later. When all her replies were ready, she sat at one end of a long table that functioned as a desk. She signed the letters with a felt-tip pen once I had shown her where to write by pointing or by placing her hand in the correct position.

There was one person who had written O'Keeffe several times and sounded quite desperate to see her. As it turned out, O'Keeffe agreed to meet this young woman at the ranch house. I was surprised, for in many ways O'Keeffe was reclusive, standoffish, and even abrasive toward admirers and the general public. Yet in this instance she was obviously pleased with this woman's persistence. When they finally met, O'Keeffe was warm and talkative, though reserved, as they spoke alone in the kitchen. Beforehand, O'Keeffe had instructed me to come get her in a half hour, thereby signaling the end of the visit.

During this period O'Keeffe began inviting me to eat lunch with her. Ida would come to where I was working, and would ask whether I'd like to join O'Keeffe. At first I was offered salad and a beverage to go with my sandwich, or some fruit, or part of the dessert, if there was one. Several days later O'Keeffe said perhaps I should plan on eating lunch with her regularly; then I would not have to pack one myself.

It strikes me now, in thinking back on that time, that O'Keeffe possessed a range of personality and physical traits which, in a peculiar way, made her visual weaknesses and advanced years seem less pronounced or even unnoticeable. Her stature, though slight, never seemed frail or diminutive, so marked and full of poise was her carriage. What I surmised, and later confirmed through old photographs of her youthful attractiveness, was drawn from features that were timeless, handsome, and pleasing in distribution. One did not mistake her age, but "old" seldom attached to "woman" when one thought of her, and the years modulated her vitalities and enthusiasms in a manner befitting her stage in life. One saw the wrinkled eye, but that feature was defined by a smile that disarmed and encouraged. Even more, the eye, blue but clouded in gray, could still size one up with authority or pathos, questioningly or icily. If the eye suffered internal impairments known only to her, outwardly it disowned its disabilities, so commanding were the settings of gesture and expression framing it.

Her voice transmitted intelligence, generosity, and candor. The lined face and nose, the bone structure softening in profile with age, the slight eyebrows arched lightly or bunched—these were animated and enhanced by the lilting cadence of her voice and its perceptible emphasis in inflection, its quavering modulation in pitch and tone due to age, and its locutions from a slightly different time.

O'Keeffe's face and gestures rewarded one's interest in her, and told one more than did words alone. When put together with the idiomatic language highly characteristic of her—revealed in letters and in some of her formal writings—the lifted eyebrow, the direct look, and the hand extended in air left the observer acutely conscious of those over-tones that are the mark of a distinctive personality. O'Keeffe showed how beauty, in one sense, is as much a matter of comportment and temperament as of age or accidents of physical endowment.

To see O'Keeffe in the way I did supposed, in retrospect, a felicitous conjunction of factors, no one of which alone ruled the rest. I arrived at a picture of her stature that was not derived from an appreciation of her art, or accomplishments, or personal history. She was someone I worked for, and, though that meant an inequality of sorts, in another sense I considered myself her equal, in terms of ideals espoused among all persons. I do not know how else to describe the immediate ease we experienced together, except that I was unaffected by those aspects of her life that distanced her from most people, namely, her accomplish-ments as an artist, and the resulting veneration of her as the artist, not the person. For me, she was a person to converse or joke with as I would with anyone else, and when she responded immediately, a tone was struck. Our relationship developed as naturally as it would if I were meeting someone with whom to share small but meaningful pleasures, or with whom a slight remark or observation would indicate depths of common interest. The smile or chuckle soon came unguarded on her part.

O'Keeffe spoke to another part of me, one that respected and admired older people, and sought them out as counselors or guides. What may have begun as a parent's injunction to respect one's elders had been confirmed for me in my relationships with parents and grandparents, teachers, writers, and others whose advanced years betokened increased sensibility and wisdom. I clearly felt the possibility of such a relationship with O'Keeffe. Her confidence, understated authority, and forthright nature struck me immediately, and my appreciation of her grew as we became more familiar with each other. It was not long before our conversations were exchanges between an older person and a younger who asked for encouragement and support.

O'Keeffe did nothing to discourage such a natural, and, given my youth and station in life, perhaps inevitable relationship. We spoke of concerns common to all people: anxiety, risk, courage, hope, failure, uncertainty, and the like. Not every conversation broached questions of what to do with my life, or how she had lived hers, but quickly the bounds of conversation and social intercourse easily exceeded the terms of our relationship as employer and employee.

We talked about hiking and books, music, the different kinds of work one could engage in, people she knew and had known in the area. For example, she lit up when I told her I often hiked along the streams around Barranco, saying I must bring her back some of the fresh watercress growing beside them. In another conversation, I mentioned to her how, while I helped my brother-in-law Jim Kempes teach pottery at a town building in Abiquiu, I had found a number of old *The New Republic* magazines with her name on the subscription label. She wanted to know if I "took" any magazines myself, and was pleased to hear I subscribed to several, wanting to know which ones. She was quite interested in my family, and in finding out how long the Polings had been involved with the Presbyterian Church as ministers in the Southwest. Such were the kinds of exchanges made possible by an association which, retrospectively, seems more providential than accidental.

Summer Days

O'Keeffe and I reminisced about our separate experiences hiking in the Abiquiu and Ghost Ranch area. I did a lot of hiking, by myself, and with my sister Lesley and her husband Jim Kempes. O'Keeffe, of course, knew almost all the places I hiked. There was a rumor that she had discovered a skeleton in a canyon not far from Abiquiu. She said she had, and felt it must be quite old. I told her of all the traces of Indian activity I had found: arrowheads, potsherds, old stone walls and dwelling areas, some with petroglyphs on the walls. O'Keeffe was particularly interested in these conversations, asking me to describe in detail places and things.

Because I was new to the area, everything seemed fresh to me, full of adventure and promise. There were no limits to where I could go, to the places I might discover, to the treasures I could pick up or admire along the way. I found O'Keeffe's houses testified to these same attitudes and enthusiasms. Walking the land was a passion she shared. At the ranch house, the outdoor shelves skirting parts of the patio were full of smooth rocks, pieces of dry wood in graceful or uncommon shapes, and clean antlers and skulls. These things were witness to O'Keeffe's affection for the country around her. Lesley, Jim, and I had collected such things long before I met O'Keeffe. We brought back treasures from our days wandering in canyons, walking on mesa tops, or following the fragile streams flowing out of the mountains that supply water to Barranco. There are few excitements to compare with finding an arrowhead, crafted hundreds of years ago, resting delicately above the ground on a slender sand pedestal, glinting smooth and shiny black against the red-stippled earth. In this country, alert and searching eyes are seldom disappointed, and often rewarded.

One day I read to O'Keeffe the conditions that governed the Stieglitz/O'Keeffe archives at the Beinecke Library at Yale. I came to a clause which, paraphrased, stipulated that certain personal correspondence shall be kept in sealed envelopes and not opened until a twenty-five-year period has passed after the death of the donor.[1] O'Keeffe chuckled to herself and then mumbled, "It's not long enough." I looked up to see whether she was going to say something more. Her left eye, twinkling, peered at me. I started to read again, only to be suddenly interrupted.

"Twenty-five years . . . *you'll* still be around," she smiled wryly.

"And you know I'll be right there to read them," I said, joining her in laughter.

More than one time she said to me, shaking her head, "I don't know how I ever got it into my head to paint." She described a painting she had seen when she was younger, showing a camel getting ready to cross some water. The water was supposed to be a large stream or river, but to O'Keeffe it looked instead like a puddle. At any rate, she continued, *that* painting certainly did not influence her. What did influence her were "the great, old river beds, where no water flowed," referring, of course, to dry riverbeds viewed from an airplane.

One weekend, O'Keeffe said one of her friends, Louise McKinney, was coming to visit her, and bringing along her daughter Robin. I knew of both of them, but, though I had met Robin when she and my sister worked at *New Mexico Magazine,* I had never met her mother.

O'Keeffe on the portal at the ranch house, surrounded by wooden shelves holding bones, wood, and rocks she had brought back from her walks in the surrounding area. Photograph © Todd Webb. Photograph © Todd Webb (b. 1905), Untitled (At the Ranch), nd, gelatin silver photograph, Todd Webb Study Collection, Museum of Fine Arts, Museum of New Mexico, Gift of Mr. and Mrs. Todd Webb.

O'Keeffe thought we should take a picnic, and had the cooks pack cold chicken and other food for the outing.

We decided to drive to the Benedictine Monastery of Christ in the Desert. O'Keeffe wanted the two of us to make the trip in my Volkswagen, which she called my "buggie." She liked my car enormously, and, as far as my experience went, in extreme disproportion to its merits. "Why," she said, "it is all a person needs." She took a peculiar enjoyment (that I never understood) from riding in it whenever possible, preferring it to her white Mercedes, the car of my obvious choice.

O'Keeffe thought she and I could lead the way for the McKinneys. We climbed in my car while Robin and her mother got in theirs. Before we could go anywhere, I had to wrestle O'Keeffe into the seat belt. I told O'Keeffe I had visions of her bouncing out of the car, and of the newspaper headlines that would describe the death of a famous artist on an obscure dirt road in northern New Mexico caused by falling out of a Volkswagen Beetle. Once O'Keeffe was belted in, her head did not come much higher than the bottom of the window in the car's door.

The road to the monastery is some twelve miles of bumps, rocks, potholes, and dirt. It follows the Chama River upriver toward Gallina Canyon. At first I drove gingerly, striving to lessen the bumpy ride for my passenger. But after a mile or so I noticed that O'Keeffe seemed to relish the bumps. Encouraged by her childish delight, I drove a bit faster. The harder bumps elicited an "Oh, my!" and a smile she unsuccessfully tried to conceal.

O'Keeffe was especially energetic that day. The subject of the monastery reminded her of meeting Thomas Merton, the famous monk and writer of numerous books on the Christian monastic life, at her home in Abiquiu, and when we returned, she gave me a copy of his *Conjectures of a Guilty Bystander*.

We did not stay long at the monastery, just long enough to get out and look at the chapel, before heading back.

Many miles after leaving the monastery we passed a dilapidated adobe house on the opposite side of the river. I pointed it out to O'Keeffe.

"Wouldn't that be a great place to live?" I said.

"That could be quite nice, couldn't it." She looked over in its general direction and then turned to me. "Why, you could just live there and paint, and do nothing else," she stated seriously. Her tone and look made my half-considered remark seem a decision away from becoming a reality.

For our lunch we drove to one of the picnic tables overlooking the Abiquiu Dam. O'Keeffe and McKinney talked, Robin and I listened, and then Robin and I visited for a few minutes off to the side. We stayed perhaps an hour before returning to the ranch house. O'Keeffe enjoyed the outing, saying to me later that she did not see friends as often as she liked. She noted resignedly that she seemed to be outliving more and more of the people she had known in her life.

O'Keeffe's consideration of my interests, and the evident pleasure she felt in sharing likes, dislikes, and essential compatibilities, solidified my enthusiasm and desire for spending as much time as possible with her. Soon I went to the ranch house on weekends as well as weekdays. When it came time to report my hours to Hamilton I recorded fewer than I actually worked, knowing he would be angry and jealous that I was spending so much time with O'Keeffe. I feared his censure because, more than anything, I wanted to continue my relationship with O'Keeffe.

O'Keeffe frequently called me in the evening after I returned home to Hamilton's house. Sometimes the calls had a stated purpose: she would remind me of something we had to be sure we got done the next day. I remember one such phone call. She called at 9:10 P.M. from the ranch house, initially addressing me as "Juan" when I picked up the phone. I reminded her that, no, my name was John, though it was Juan in Spanish. She laughed lightly and corrected herself. I was going to Santa Fe the next day, and since I was leaving directly from Hamilton's house, she called to add a few more things to the list: I was to get salt at the co-op and some large planter pots at the nursery.

O'Keeffe sounded pleasantly tired, the tone of her voice warm. I began to fabricate an absurd story about her. I do not remember exactlly what I said, but soon she was in stitches. As her laughter subsided, she became quiet, and paused. She had been outside in the night, she said, just prior to our phone conversation, and described the night as being "very simple in the blue. It was warm, and windy, and very soft to me." She could see the stars. Nothing more than these things was needed, she said. I was oddly overwhelmed when she hung up.

During the summer there were several visitors to the O'Keeffe households. Her sister Claudia came with her maid. She and O'Keeffe got together regularly for meals. On occasion, I drove Claudia to Santa Fe, and waited for her outside the more fashionable stores while she shopped. On one such trip O'Keeffe asked me to buy her some stockings at The Guarantee, a store on the plaza, an experience I found somewhat awkward, and which O'Keeffe, when I told her of it, found endlessly amusing. Another visitor O'Keeffe enjoyed considerably was the writer Gerald Sykes. Before he arrived, O'Keeffe pulled out one of his books, *The Hidden Remnant*, and had me read from it to her, later giving it to me when she saw my interest in it.

I often talked about music with O'Keeffe. I played electric guitar intermittently with various bands while I lived in Barranco. I was preoccupied with music, unable to resolve my intentions with and seriousness about it, and willing to postpone any decision now that I was faced with the possibility of working with O'Keeffe. She listened patiently, commenting only that it was very difficult to live the life of a musician.

Recently I had purchased an album titled *Black Market* by a group called Weather Report. I was so taken by the album that I told O'Keeffe about it and wondered whether she would like to hear it. She agreed. I brought the album to the Abiquiu house one day, and, after lunch and her rest, I played the title track. She sat in a reclining chair facing two black speakers of modern design, very thin and with a slight curve. While the record played, she listened intently with her eyes closed.

When it was done she opened her eyes, paused reflectively, then said: "That was very good. It moved like this," and her right hand gestured rhythmically in the air, marking the beat. "It . . . it has a flow . . . ," she began, and then quickly cut herself off as she found the words she was after.

"It has a certain feel to it that . . . that's like a wave." Her voice began higher in pitch on "wave" and descended as she drew out the vowel. This time her hand represented differently the shape of the music, rising gently up and down as it moved from right to left. I played a few of the other compositions from the album, but none elicited the same response as the first piece.

On August 7, 1976, O'Keeffe was invited to a premiere performance of Virgil Thomson's *The Mother of Us All* at the Santa Fe Opera.[2] The plans for the evening included dinner, followed by the opera, which most likely we would not see in its entirety. When O'Keeffe and I first talked about the evening several weeks in advance, she expressed her concern that the whole affair sounded tiring. She was not looking forward to it. A friend of hers—it was unclear to me whether that friend was Thomson or the producer of the opera in Santa Fe—was involved, and she felt obligated to attend.

The afternoon preceding the event, the Abiquiu household bustled with activity. I arrived before 4:00 P.M., when the scurrying about was at a peak. I could not see what was going on when I entered O'Keeffe's studio area, but I knew Mary and Ida were getting O'Keeffe dressed, fixing her hair, and so on, behind the partially closed bathroom door at the end of the studio. I heard voices and movement.

Finally, O'Keeffe emerged from the bathroom and carefully stepped down the few stairs to the studio level. She took a few steps toward me, then paused, cane in one hand, a smile faint across closed lips. O'Keeffe looked quite handsome. Her hair was piled in circles on her head differently than usual. She wore a tightly woven gray skirt with matching jacket; the material seemed to shimmer, a trace of blue in the suit's weave. Under her jacket she wore a simple white blouse pinned at the neck with the ever-present Calder "OK." She exuded self-conscious pleasure with her appearance. It was the first time in months that she had dressed for a special occasion. For several moments she stood before me. She looked very sharp, and, unabashedly, I told her so.

It was early yet, so I read her mail to her before our departure. There was a letter from Gerald Sykes; one from John Smythers, her tax man with the firm of Webster and Sheffield; and a letter from Doris Bry. The last was not opened; O'Keeffe said to save it for Juan. At 5:15 P.M., we left for Santa Fe in the Mercedes.

At this time of day in summer, driving away from the sun, light strikes the land in a way that reveals the mesa country afresh. The intensity of the midday sun is past, and the land offers a slightly different array of colors and shapes. Dark blue and purple shadows mark cuts in the hills, emphasizing their features in unexpected ways. Contours are enhanced by shadows, colors, and hues that accompany the arc of the sun through the summer sky. On clear days, shadows in the Sangre de Cristo Mountains, over fifty miles to the east, seem cooling, even at such remove.

We drove for awhile in silence, O'Keeffe's eyes shrouded in large sunglasses, incongruous in style ("pseudo-Aspen," I'd call them) and size. She began talking again of traveling to the "lost cities." She said she preferred Machu Picchu and Angkor Wat, as well as others in southern India, whose names she did not remember, to the great modern cities, which never appealed to her in the same way.

We drove in silence before she began describing a dream she had had recently. It was in color, and she felt "ageless." In it a young boy was walking along a path carrying an umbrella. She followed, carrying a chair and a shovel. They were traveling in a large, triangular pattern, and, after some time, came to a gate, where the boy left his umbrella. She looked ahead and saw him far up on a hill. A woman also stood there, looking down at her quietly. The woman reminded O'Keeffe of the Project HOPE nurses[3] who waited for the ship to come in. O'Keeffe could not make out the woman's demeanor. O'Keeffe smiled at me, and said that in the dream she wished she did not have to carry all that gear.

By 6:15 we reached the bottom of the hill near the opera house. At the entrance to a new land development adjoining the opera, we met John Crosby, founder of the Santa Fe Opera, Bill Katz, and three other gentlemen who were friends of Crosby's. We drove with Crosby to the proposed site of an O'Keeffe museum on one of the highest points outside Santa Fe, nearly seven thousand feet high. We climbed higher and higher, and from the back seat of the car the plains toward Española and Abiquiu seemed very far away. Nothing but piñon and juniper surrounded us. We could see much of the Española valley and a hint of the mesas on the way toward Taos. The others claimed that Pedernal was visible, but I could not make it out.

After ten minutes we continued to a picnic area. I helped O'Keeffe out of the car. She slipped her hand round my arm, and, slowly, we followed the others up a sandy incline to a table set for dinner out in the open. To the east were the Sangre de Cristo Mountains, to the west the Jemez Mountains, some features of each obscured by clouds. Scrubby trees framed our dinner table. During dinner, O'Keeffe and Crosby reminisced about their experiences in the Southwest. Crosby was friendly and bright in a quiet way.

The conversation had much to do with Crosby and others offering a site for the museum. O'Keeffe was interested, but restrained and non-committal; she said many of the details must wait until Juan returned from New York.

We sat almost until the time for the opera to begin, then drove back to the opera house and followed Crosby and the others to our seats near the front of the house. When O'Keeffe and I walked down the aisle heads turned, and whispers could be heard.

Our seats were excellent. I took O'Keeffe's hand and guided her to the third row. Once we were seated, O'Keeffe put a scarf on her head and a shawl over her shoulders. The effect was striking.

The first act was long. During the intermission, I went for my jacket and brought the car to the front. The second act moved more quickly. As we left, O'Keeffe held my arm. She surprised me as we exited by pumping hands and smiling graciously and warmly all the way to the car.

Instead of driving through Española, I took the road through San Juan Pueblo. The road winds through the old pueblo and dips through the bosque. A one-lane bridge crosses the Chama River. I opened the overhead panel in the car to the cool evening air. Stars crowded the sky; the moon lit the land, casting stark shadows in the night.

O'Keeffe talked about the museum idea; she liked it, but was put off by all the details, and was not at all sure about the location. She felt she would be consumed by the project. It would entail countless decisions for her, she said wearily. It would be easier if her eyes were better. She repeated phrases, now familiar to me, about her former vision.

O'Keeffe was unusually talkative that evening and jumped from one topic to another. She talked of the more than one hundred pictures of her taken by Stieglitz that no one had ever seen. For the first time in my presence, she referred to him as "my husband," and used the phrase many times on the way home. As we detoured through San Juan, we talked of music and its peculiar demands. The moonlit landscape reminded her of hiking all night when she was younger. We drove on, talking, through the night.

Once we reached Abiquiu, we went into the kitchen. Pita Lopez (the daughter of Candelaria Lopez, one of the day-cooks), who sometimes worked for O'Keeffe as a companion, and Mary Grether were asleep in the studio. O'Keeffe was not ready for bed yet. She said we should have something to eat, and told me to get cheese and bread out of the refrigerator. I was about to do so when she interrupted me.

"Oh, but we best wash our hands." She shuffled over to the sink. "Think of all those people's hands we've been shaking. Now, come on," she motioned, "you too!"

"That sounds like something my mother would say," I replied.

"Oh," she chuckled, as if I had said something scandalous, and I moved next to her at the sink.

Afterwards, with clean hands, we enjoyed our late-night snack.

After dinner one night in Abiquiu I accompanied O'Keeffe back to her bedroom. It was the time of summer when thunderheads spring up during the day and often linger into the evening. If one has a commanding enough view of the countryside, showers are visible at great distances, a perfect illustration of the random and unpredictable nature of summer rain in northern New Mexico. Great, dense sheets of gray-black mist move without sound across mesas far away, in and out of canyons and valleys, sometimes trailing long virgas, streamers of rain that never reach the earth. Just as quickly, these showers end, and the storm's faint rumble and an occasional flicker of lightning deep within the thunderhead are the only reminders of rain as the storm moves on.

Many times it rained high up in the hills in back of Mesa Montosa, behind the ranch house, while the flats down by the house remained clear and dry. We knew nonetheless of high mountain showers, for suddenly water would appear on the cliffs. Long, plunging spouts of muddy water would run off the tall cliffs for ten or fifteen minutes before the flow lessened to a trickle, then disappeared.

That evening in Abiquiu the air seemed charged with something urgent and compelling. An abrupt wind heightened the feeling of expectation. It was well after 7 P.M. O'Keeffe and I were looking out of her bedroom window at the sky when the clouds took on vibrant, pastel-like colors from the rays of the sun setting to the west.

"Look at those clouds!" I exclaimed, waving broadly with my arm at the expanse of sky outside.

O'Keeffe came closer to the window. I knew she wanted to retire, and I was ready to leave. Wind-whipped bushes twisted wildly outside the window. Sand sprayed against the glass with a stippled, erratic sound.

"I've got to go outside," I said.

I opened the door and went out, followed by O'Keeffe. We stood in a swirling wind which seemed to blow in every direction. Above and to the east were low and swollen clouds; the air smelled of rain mingled pungently with the scent of sagebrush. Clouds roiled overhead, lacking clearly defined shapes or edges. It was impossible to tell if they were moving toward us or away from us.

Most striking of all was the intensity of color dusting the clouds.

"What are those colors?" I asked, shouting over the wind.

O'Keeffe raised her eyes skyward, resting both hands on the cane. She looked slowly all around, squinting against the flying sand, her white dress flapping loudly. Then she lowered her eyes toward me.

"You tell me what they are," she said.

At first I thought she was jesting. I knew she could see them, or I thought she could. But she waited patiently, looking at me. I turned back to the sky.

"They're like pastels." I stopped, focusing on one cloud closer to us.

"This cloud is like a grainy orange and red—no, it's more like a peach—with yellows in there, too." I gestured widely. It seemed as if one color was superimposed on traces of another. The air was full of fragrances enhanced by a hint of moisture and sharpened by the wind as it passed quickly over the surface of sage and stone, sand and piñon. Somehow, all that was part of what I saw.

"But there are reds, too." I struggled to think of how to describe the colors. "There is a gray or white behind the reds; and some orange." O'Keeffe's head declined slightly as she listened, her lips creased in a faint smile. The momentary nature of the storm, the darker clouds as backdrop for those other clouds tinted in soft pastels overhead, the clearing sky far to the west, the turbulent gray-blacks on the horizon line to the east—how to describe those features to her? I gestured futilely.

"How would you paint that?" I finally exclaimed. "Could you capture that?" She laughed at me and let my remarks pass.

We stood silently for some time until the wind began to subside. It never did rain. The clouds scudded to the east, and the sky began to clear as the light and color noiselessly dissipated.

Several days later O'Keeffe gave me a set of pastels which she thought I should try.

"How do you use these?" I asked. The wooden box was large and contained a seemingly endless array of colors.

She looked up at me and said bluntly: "You'll just have to find out for yourself."

It was quiet for a moment. I was dissatisfied with her reply.

"Well," I tried again, "do you use your fingers, or a tissue, or cloth of some kind, to blend or smooth them?"

She seemed to take an obscure pleasure in not answering me directly.

"Oh, you'll see," she said, gesturing loosely with one hand. "Just try some different things."

Over the next several evenings I made swaths of color, just broad bands, trying to recreate those from the night before. I attempted to ease one color into another. When I showed them to O'Keeffe she encouraged me to "keep at it." Shortly after Hamilton returned to stay, in September, his work in New York completed, she angrily asked me for the pastels, as though she were suspicious of me.

The Patio

One morning, as I was priming the outside trim, Mary Grether came out and said O'Keeffe needed my help. I followed Mary into the studio, but not until I had wrapped my paint brush in a cloth dampened with thinner; I never knew how long I would be away on such occasions. O'Keeffe and Mary were looking at a white canvas, around four feet by six feet, which they had resting on an easel.

"We put a coat of primer on this several days ago," O'Keeffe said. "Mary says the white isn't even." I, too, noticed inconsistencies in the white primer coat: the cream colored canvas showed through the paint in many places. O'Keeffe gestured toward the canvas. Her left hand rested, in her typical fashion, upside down on her hip.

"The primer *must* be even. Do you think you can put on another thin coat? Have you ever painted before?"

"Only a paint-by-the-numbers set when I was very young," I said, tongue in cheek, "and what I'm doing outside."

"Then you never have painted," she said, smiling. She and Mary showed me the paint, gum turpentine, assorted containers, brushes, palette knives, and mixing tools. Mary left to attend to other duties.

O'Keeffe directed me to a work table. Some primer was already mixed in a wide, low can, something like a two-pound coffee can cut in two.

"Take some of the lead white and squeeze it in there. You must be careful not to get too much of it on you. The old-style paint used to have lead in it, and some of these tubes are quite old." I squeezed out a quarter of a tube.

"Now, take one of these sticks here and stir it. We'll have to add some turpentine."

She leaned over the work table and found the shape of a tall cylinder of turpentine. After removing the top, she moved the can slowly toward the mixing can. Then, entirely by feel, she gently poured two quick splashes of turpentine into the paint.

"There. Now try that."

I stirred the mixture slowly. The consistency she wanted was not very thick; it was only an undercoat to cover the canvas. At one point, she took the stick in hand, testing the thickness of the paint by feeling its resistance against the stick. When she was satisfied the primer was ready, she told me to apply it with a large brush. I put the brush in the paint and began to apply it to the canvas. I asked her how thick the coat should be.

"Those patches have to be covered. You don't want bare canvas showing through." I continued to ask her questions, simple ones about how long the paint took to dry, how soon one could paint over it, whether she primed a number of canvases in advance, and so on.

After fifteen minutes, she left, saying I should come get her when I finished.

Once alone, I deferred to the undercurrent of anticipation marked for me by this new activity, still unaware of my degree of involvement. I knew only how significant a departure it was from the work I had done up to that time.

The primer was left to dry over the weekend. When I drove to the ranch Monday morning, I learned O'Keeffe and Mary had been fussing with the canvas. They invited me into the studio.

"I want to draw a line with charcoal along the top here," said O'Keeffe. The anticipation I felt the Friday before now lurched in my chest, together with a sudden admixture of apprehension and excitement, which was only exaggerated by O'Keeffe's relaxed attitude. Mary left us.

"How far down do you want it?" I asked.

"Oh, I think something like this." Her hand loosely suggested a ten- or twelve-inch width from the top.

I measured several marks with a yardstick at regular intervals, and then, with a small piece of charcoal, lightly drew a line across the top of the canvas. I did not know what kind of painting she had in her head; I do not think she wanted me to know at that time either. She moved close to the line, trying to gauge the width of the band and get a sense of its relation to the rest of the canvas. She seemed satisfied.

"Now, what this needs is some blue along the top. Just a long blue band." Again she waved her hand in the direction of the canvas. Her eyes held mine as if I should appreciate this information. She turned away from me to the work table. "Mary and I have some paints out on the table." There were many small boxes which held tubes of paint; some were open. Several tubes of blue were clustered together.

"I want the blue, the cerulean blue," she said, elongating the "ru" in "cerulean." "There's a glass plate and some palette knives there. Squeeze some out on the glass and stir it up."

I squeezed out coils of the cerulean paint. Then she asked for one of the palette knives. She used it to flatten out the paint, pushing it around in circles until it was of a more uniform texture and consistency. After a few moments, she handed me the knife and told me to do the same. Soon there was a thin layer of paint covering five or six inches of the glass.

We took the glass palette, knife, paint, and several smaller paintbrushes to the canvas. O'Keeffe repeatedly felt the bristles on first one brush, then another. Finally finding one she liked, perhaps three-quarters of an inch wide, she leaned close to the palette and began pushing it into the paint. Then she turned back to the canvas and started painting.

She painted quickly, almost pushing the paint into the canvas. I watched quietly. Her movements appeared authoritative and practiced.

Her left hand rested on her hip; her right moved regularly from palette to canvas. But, after a few minutes, I noticed something amiss. She dipped the brush in the paint on the glass palette even when there was already enough paint on the brush. Sometimes she painted the same small area twice, and left the paint thick and rough on the surface. Then she might continue several inches away, thinking that she was where she had left off. I had an odd feeling: her brush movements should have produced something significantly different from what appeared on the canvas. I realized she must have made those movements by habit, from memory.

As I watched her it was as if I were observing both O'Keeffe and myself from a distance. There was the direct and forceful impression of watching an accomplished artist practicing her art as few had been privileged to do. It seemed that, if I could only watch and remember carefully enough, something deeper and not quite visible to the eye might become apparent, some insight would be given, some clue to art. I wondered that I should be in the position of observer when O'Keeffe had worked in solitude throughout her life. I did not know where to stand, and moved back and to one side, feeling uncertain about my presence and my role there.

It was not the first time that day nor that summer when I felt I was both participant and observer in this world made by Georgia O'Keeffe, sometimes marveling at circumstances and events and wondering how long they could last, at other times utterly preoccupied with the work at hand.

After several minutes she asked me how far she was from the charcoal line.

What was asked outstripped my abilities. I was uncertain about saying anything, and immediately felt how my words would speak to more than O'Keeffe's ability to paint to a line. I felt in her question more than what I heard. There was a clear trace of resignation, even lack of confidence, in her tone that was matched by the way her whole face was uplifted slightly toward mine. The light thumping of brush against canvas made it easy for each of us, one in imagination, the other in memory, to place that sound to numerous, distant occasions. I could not help but see the marked unevenness of the canvas before us, and to place it in contrast against the history of her accomplishment, made possible by a keen and sound eye, an eye now attenuated with age and refusing to serve otherwise undiminished artistic capacities.

Moreover, I was still unclear as to the exact nature of her visual acuity, and did not know whether she had painted recently, or whether she had painted before with another's assistance. The newness of the activity, coupled with my ignorance not only of painting, but of what painting meant to O'Keeffe at this stage in her life, made it seem as though anything I might say would be utterly groundless and without justification. What did I know about painting, let alone about living and the world, when compared to her?

I decided that candor was the best policy: I would tell her exactly what I saw, pointing out first what she had accomplished, and then, more gently, describing the imperfections, all the while avowing my own uncertainty at this unfamiliar task. My hesitation, which was so pronounced internally to me, seemed less noticeable to O'Keeffe.

"I don't know if you want it this way or not, but the paint is very thick here,"—I indicated a general area—"and there is white primer showing through over here," I said, pointing out some of the patchy spots by way of comparison with those areas that were more even.

"We can't have that." She tried to fix those areas, asking me whether she was in the right place. After a few minutes of my patiently pointing and explaining, she seemed to grow weary.

"I think you'd better do it," she sighed, looking at me almost wistfully. That was all she said. Her voice was tired; she sounded disappointed in a remote way, but seemed to accept her situation unhesitatingly. The brush was in my hand. I was supposed to start painting as readily as she had ceased doing so.

Suddenly I had many questions. How thick did she want the paint? What about the top and sides, should they be painted too? What happened if you painted over the tacks holding the canvas on the stretcher? The paint did not cover the canvas easily or evenly. I became obsessed with the importance of a perfectly even application. Doing the job with her standing by seemed overwhelming. In contrast, O'Keeffe exuded a kind of calm pleasure at my sudden preoccupations, while welcoming the attention I was giving to painting.

"The paint's a little thick here. Should I just brush it around?"

"If it's too thick, then you take a palette knife and scrape it off. That's all."

As I painted, she continued to stand by me, watching in silence. It took some time before I had painted enough to establish my own makeshift standard of comparison, shaped by the questions I put to her. But ten minutes of painting, even with a single color that applied easily enough, was nothing to go on. My prior uneasiness at remarking on her painting and my fear of seeming presumptuous was newly accentuated; in this context especially, I could not escape the presence of the woman standing beside me, nor elude the expectations of the moment, self-imposed or otherwise.

Yet, whatever the misgivings I had, whatever shape they took, they were known in some measure to O'Keeffe. For most of that day and often in the days following I struggled with the knowledge I knew we shared. Her achievements in painting, and my inexperience with this domain of the visual arts, could have overwhelmed either or both of us, and made the undertaking seem jejune and incapable of meaningful result. Part of O'Keeffe's accomplishment in working with me was creating an environment wherein we could function in concert with each other. It is astounding to me how comfortable O'Keeffe made me feel, and the extent to which I was treated as a genuine collaborator in the projects we undertook. O'Keeffe's encouragement ensured that I was a participant from the outset, and that I was never immobilized by too constant reflection on the disparities and contrasts everywhere evident.

Each conversational exchange, each suggestion or piece of instruction that day and later, was surrounded with good will and accommodation, and grounded on the assumption that I could do what needed to be done.

I continued painting, and the blue gradually began to cover the top of the canvas. Periodically I stopped to mix more paint.

"Are you getting close to the line?" she asked.

I was, but I had avoided painting up to it. She went to the work table and felt the ends of some smaller brushes. She brought me two or three, suggesting I try one. Painting to the line went much slower. She asked me how it was going and whether I liked the brush I was using, encouraging me to try any size I wanted.

When I had painted about a quarter of the way across the top of the canvas, O'Keeffe introduced me to a new brush and a new technique. The new brush was kept in its own box. She seemed to treasure it in a particular way, and when I began to use it, she told me always to handle it with great care and clean it thoroughly. It was a large, thick brush, of a kind she said was not readily available; this one she'd had for many, many years. It was used only after paint had already been applied.

Working almost solely from her sense of touch, she showed me how to brush the surface of the canvas gently to smooth out the ridges and the rough texture in the paint left by brush marks. This technique could also be used to soften transitions from one color to another. She stood with her back to me, her left hand inverted on her hip, her right carefully executing the motions she wanted me to duplicate.

Ever so lightly, she brushed the area I had painted, her arm moving from left to right, covering a three- to four-inch area with each pass. It was as if she dusted the paint with air. I began to get the idea. It was very important, she said, to stop often and clean the brush so that paint did not build up on the bristles and make them stiff. She used a paper towel lightly moistened with gum turpentine to wipe off the paint; another towel was used to dry off the brush. Later, I added another step, brushing a third, clean towel, to be sure there were no traces of paint left. It was a painstaking and time-consuming task for an area of any size, but she insisted on doing it this way: it produced the kind of finish and texture she demanded.

Several days later O'Keeffe taught me how to shade one color into another. Where one color is painted to the border of the other, a clean brush, roughly stroked back and forth along the line, mixes the two. Finally, a large brush—what I called the "finishing" brush—accomplishes a range of gentle transformations in texture and shade, from one color, to an intermediate shade, to the second color. O'Keeffe demonstrated each of these steps before having me replicate them.

That morning was exhilarating for both of us. I think she enjoyed it for two reasons. The immediate one was that an idea she had for a painting was being realized on canvas. Even at this early stage, her face showed enthusiasm and pleasure with the whole business surrounding painting. I had never seen this in her before, and painting was clearly tonic to her overall well-being. Though initially she knew nothing about my ability as a painter, she knew from observation that I was good with my hands, and at no point was my lack of preparation an obstacle for her. In fact, she told me she wanted someone who had no painting experience prior to working with her, and hence had no ideas about how to paint. She had tried painting with Hamilton as she and I had painted, but she said it was too difficult for them to work together. "He had too many ideas that got in the way," she said, and they abandoned the possibility. Besides, O'Keeffe recognized and approved of the attention brought to other tasks I had completed for her.

A second source of her pleasure was my enthusiasm, as untutored and spontaneous as it was. As I pushed and brushed the paint around the canvas I began to see how wonderful painting could be—and I was only applying a single color! "How neat!" I would blurt out, or, "Just look at that!" A long, bold swath of cerulean blue set off strikingly the white below. "No wonder you like painting so much," I said, half-facetiously, knowing how much more was involved in painting than I was aware of. To all these remarks she responded with delight, chuckling at my primitive and unreflective fervor.

For O'Keeffe there was an obvious, childlike enjoyment in having the tools of painting around. When I remarked to her that I liked the smell of turpentine and paint she smiled quickly, and confessed she did also. Even if she was not able to engage in the whole business of painting as she had before, O'Keeffe took great pleasure in the pleasures I discovered, whether simple ones, such as the feel of paint on a glass palette under a palette knife, or of a brush on canvas, or more complex ones, such as seeing emerge on the canvas the end to which the artist's materials were directed.

When I had finished the band at the end of the day, we stood back from the canvas. There was not much to see but the brilliant, inviting contrast of white and blue.

"Well, that's something." Her eyes looked at me with evident satisfaction.

"Yes," I replied. "I *like* that."

What we had painted thus far was like the anticipation of some wonderful secret; it was as if O'Keeffe knew the secret and took pleasure in withholding it from me, knowing I would soon know what it was, and wondering if I might guess it before the painting was completed. And from the manner in which the secret was withheld, I knew she assumed, rightly, that I would be equally pleased.

The next morning I went straight to the studio. O'Keeffe came in from her bedroom after I called out. She asked me how I was, and we chatted for a few minutes. She was lively and eager to get under way with our work.

Today, she said, we were going to draw a large square in the middle, again using charcoal and the yardstick. She and Mary had put out some tubes of yellow ocher paint.

Turning to the canvas, she said: "I think our blue looks quite fine, don't you?"

I agreed. "Maybe we should leave it as it is," I said. "It makes a great painting just like that." She chuckled.

Her concern that day was with the square in the center. She asked me how the light was where we had positioned the easel, parallel to a short wall ending by the door to the patio. The light coming into the room was direct at this early hour; it glanced off the surface of the canvas. From late morning on, most of the light in the studio was indirect; by the end of the day it reflected off the towering sandstone cliffs several hundred feet in back of the house. I moved the canvas so that it angled slightly toward the fireplace, diagonal to the tall windows. The gray and yellow cliffs were still in shadow out beyond.

I began experimenting with the size of the square, which I drew and re-drew several times. O'Keeffe's eyesight made it difficult to convey to her its precise position. I gestured with the yardstick or with my arm, holding either one in place while she scrutinized its position. I would draw a light charcoal line wherever she wanted a part of the square, using a paper tissue to brush away lines that had to be changed. O'Keeffe often came up to the canvas, one hand gently touching the surface, as if her touch would show her what her eyes could not. The blue was easily visible—she could see that. But small, thin charcoal lines were not. She could not tell exactly where they ended, and, clearly, the proportions were crucial. We managed, though, and eventually settled on the size.

Before I mixed the paint, O'Keeffe asked me to check something about the color we would be using that day—yellow ocher—in a book on painting with oils.[1] It was an old book, and it contained a section describing the basic colors and noting the compatibility of their qualities and tones in relation to other colors. When I had finished consulting the book, she said, as if to herself, "That's all right then."

"I suppose you know all about these colors," I remarked, flipping through the pages of the book.

"Well, you *have* to." She paused before turning toward me. "The first thing you learn is what colors go with other ones. You learn all that and get it out of the way, so you can paint."

"So you learn the techniques first?" I asked.

"Well . . . *yes*," she said with a slight hesitation. Her emphasis conveyed agreement of a qualified kind, as though there were other, unspoken, considerations as well.

I prepared a portion of paint on the glass palette, spreading and smoothing out the ridges with a palette knife. Ocher looked anything but yellow; more of a shade of brown, I thought. O'Keeffe wanted to try applying the paint around the square. She found a brush and loaded it with paint, and, with it, she pushed paint into the canvas as much as brushed it across the surface. I told her what sections she was missing as she worked with the yellow ocher. Some areas were too thick, so much so that the pattern made by the canvas underneath the paint was obscured. When I made her aware of this she attempted to remedy it. Often her touch, though sure, was so light that a thick patch of paint or an inconsistency in its application remained.

As she came to the charcoal line marking off the square, I told her how many inches she was from its edge. Her motions instantly changed, the brush strokes became shorter. She painted as if she were following along a line, yet her uneven edge of paint was a good three or four inches from the line. After five minutes or so of painting like that, knowing that she was far from the mark, she said: "You can do it now."

I now realize I was watching her come up against her eyesight. She was determined to paint again although her vision was failing. Yet, remarkably, when she got to a certain point, she seemed to accept, readily, even matter-of-factly, her shortcoming.

Not all of the ocher background was painted that day. The color was difficult to apply evenly. It seemed thin in some areas, and white primer showed through, while in other places the paint was too thick. I worked diligently to apply an even coat, scraping off paint from thick areas that had been built up by either of us.

After I had done a small area, O'Keeffe suggested I use the big brush. The results, I was discovering, were dramatic. I imitated her motions with the brush, asking her as I painted what she wanted the area to look like. The brushed areas looked flatter, reflecting less "shine" than those yet untouched. Ridges and uneven areas were feathered into adjoining surfaces. I particularly enjoyed this part of painting. Using this brush on a single color was an excellent, repetitive way to practice the technique. One's touch had to be light and deft, softly stroking the paint.

It was not until that day, when we drew the large square, that I recognized we were working on something similar to O'Keeffe's Patio Door paintings. An earlier one hung in her studio, on the other side of the half wall near her bedroom. During the days we painted, I studied *White Patio with Red Door* for long periods. I examined closely her brush work to see how she feathered a color or shaded a hue; I noted the ways in which the primer coat was covered lightly to allow nuance; I studied her lines, comparing an area close-up to the effect the same area produced at a distance. Then I would shift my vision to see the picture as a whole, as if seeing the painting for the first time, trying not to be aware of those technical features from the artist's point of view. This was how I began to develop a sense of the relation between the techniques of painting and the picture an artist finally presented to the viewer.

As we continued, O'Keeffe gave me a sense of what she wanted to achieve in an area or in the painting as a whole. My task was to effect this on canvas in any way I could, and she gave me the freedom to play with the painter's tools. The time spent alone, simply completing, for example, the background of a painting, allowed me to define my own ways of accomplishing the effects observed in her paintings.

I learned to convey to her the way the texture of the canvas showed through the paint, or how quickly or slowly one color moved into another, just as I learned to gauge what she wanted. She processed the descriptive information I gave through the knowledge embedded in her memory, and held up the result against the idea she sought to realize. Painting with someone was new to her. It forced her to rethink her techniques and convey them to me so I could realize the picture she wanted. This method added a second creative aspect to that of painting, that is, the translation and conveying of knowledge and skills that were second nature to her into a form accessible to me. She found herself again at eighty-nine in the position of teacher, a position she had occupied at the beginning of her career.[2]

We developed a constant give-and-take. I asked questions and described what I saw; she made suggestions. How crucial was it to apply the paint initially? I had to cover the white primer, she said, but could also smooth out the paint with a series of finishing brushes. What size brush should I use for painting a large area of the same color? She smiled and said I should experiment, gesturing towards one of several tin cans and long, glove-sized boxes which held a staggering array of brushes. How long should I paint before using the finishing brush? She said I could work for a longer period with oils because they dried more slowly. However, she usually stopped me in my initial application of paint after twenty or thirty minutes, and encouraged me to smooth the painted surfaces, working both on the newly applied paint as well as on bringing adjacent areas together. But constantly there was an air of "Let's try this," or "Just go ahead and do it." I felt free to make mistakes and explore the uses of these new tools.

O'Keeffe's patience as a teacher, and the relaxed manner in which she taught, helped dissolve many of my anxieties. She never tired of my questions. Her explanations and manner made painting immediately accessible to me. It was, however, hard work, especially since it was unfamiliar and was transpiring under exceptional circumstances. My desire to achieve perfection was in large part self-imposed, a feature of my personality, but it was additionally governed by the quality of O'Keeffe's work and my desire to please her.

Painting gave me an appropriate opportunity to relax around O'Keeffe, for it provided us with the ideal activity as a focus for our time together. From the outset, she wanted my opinion and input. Her ideas were conveyed sparingly. The great looseness in her manner freed me to make mistakes and correct them, to offer suggestions and start over again.

None of this could have taken place without the time spent together in the previous weeks. To work with O'Keeffe required more than a minimum facility with one's hands or a primitive receptivity to art. There had to be compatibilities on another level, ones that had to be apparent and predictable by the time we began painting. The simple tasks previously done with her were the means of becoming acquainted, of exchanging likes and dislikes, and ultimately of becoming her friend. Not surprisingly, painting gave me access to a side of O'Keeffe she seldom shared with anyone else.

Within her household, it marked a complete change from the amount and kind of work I had done before: if I could paint with her, then I could do anything else as well. Painting together both presupposed the companionship of the previous weeks, and suddenly compressed the time usually required in coming to know another person intimately. The more I was with O'Keeffe, the more we distanced ourselves from the traditional employer/employee relationship that had first characterized our contact. The changes of that summer, however, would have been inconceivable, as subsequent events demonstrated, if Hamilton had not been gone.

Morning was the best time for us to work. O'Keeffe was brighter and more energetic then than later in the day, although she sat most of the morning while I painted. Lunch and a rest period followed. Then we would resume at two or half past two, working often until half past five or six o'clock. She wanted to proceed steadily once something began to take shape. By the end of the day I was exhausted. I welcomed the offer of dinner, and we sat quietly, both tired but satisfied.

O'Keeffe often stood beside me when I painted. If I seemed to be going along all right—that is, if I asked few questions—she usually sat to the side and slightly behind me. We talked regularly, though our conversation reflected O'Keeffe's economy of words. Other times, O'Keeffe sat outside on the patio, reclining on a padded chair under the cool overhang, a light wrap covering her legs. From the patio she could see Pedernal, whose presence even at a distance seems to draw to itself the surrounding country. She rested, preoccupied with her thoughts. Sometimes I found her sitting in the small eating area off the kitchen. A banco, covered with a pad and assorted cushions and pillows, ran along the wall. She sat there, a small table in front of her, facing two large picture windows. The cliffs loomed large through the north window, red hills and the ranch road disappearing through the window looking east.

She remarked to me more than once, "I always had such good eyes, such good vision." Her fingers would come together as if reaching for a detail or some small object, or showing me a very fine point in the air. Her eyes squinted. "I could see great distances," she said, the "great" gently inflected.

One day, after sketching with a small piece of charcoal, no more than a half-inch long by an eighth of an inch thick, I set it down on a black table, an all-purpose work area. I noted where I placed the charcoal, next to some papers, because otherwise it could have been easily lost to sight. O'Keeffe and I had been talking about lines on the canvas. I asked her what she could see. She turned to the picture windows, toward the cliffs and Mesa Montosa rising high above them. Large shapes she could make out: she could see, she said, where the rocks ended and the blue began. Her hand suggested the line through the glass. She turned toward the canvas: she said she could sometimes make out the charcoal lines, but not clearly or easily. Then she moved toward the black table, scanning its surface for several moments. Suddenly and unerringly, she picked up the piece of charcoal!

"It's like there are little holes in my vision," she said. "I can't see straight on very well. But around the edge there are little holes where I can see quite clearly."

The next day O'Keeffe wanted to bring the yellow ocher close to the bottom of the canvas. Later, she said we would draw in small rectangles or steps along the bottom; for now, it was enough to leave room for them. The paint still looked uneven to me. I went over some of the areas where the yellow ocher was thin.

"This should be very red here." O'Keeffe pointed to the center square. "We can start by mixing some orange, yellow, and red."

The color I mixed wasn't right. She eyed the palette intently. I made some adjustments, then mixed it again, spreading the paint over the glass so she could see it better. When she thought it seemed right, I began applying it. I painted only the bottom third of the square. We added more red, and I applied it alongside and above the first color. To blend the two I took another clean brush, and worked rapidly the area between the two colors. Soon there was a rough blend of the two shades. Again, I removed brush strokes with the large finishing brush. The final coat of red, to cover the upper third of the square, was applied over these two colors. It hung over the center of the square and surrounded the more orange area. As the final coat came down the sides it tapered to a finer and finer point, almost vanishing near the bottom of the square.

The effect of these first colors was striking. O'Keeffe could see how it looked and was invigorated by it. It was as if the burning core of a fire had been transferred to the canvas. Color arched in the center; the brown surrounding the center square seemed almost unable to contain the fire within. And over it all shone the blue. Though the painting was far from complete, it was arresting. Later that day she showed it to Ida and Mary.

When I saw the painting the next morning, I was immediately struck by the way the orange and red added movement to the painting —that is the only way to describe its effect. The viewer's eye shifted continually from the center of the painting up to the blue and back again to the center, which was enfolded by the brown. The simplicity of the composition was stunning.

When I walked into the studio, O'Keeffe and Mary were near the painting. O'Keeffe smiled at me.

"Mary and I were just admiring our painting," she said. "She thinks it's quite fine." O'Keeffe seemed almost proud.

Mary thought it was tremendous, especially since I had never painted before. I was as amazed as she was, and having O'Keeffe take such pleasure in what we were doing gave me a deep satisfaction. Mary excused herself, and O'Keeffe looked over the canvas for a few more minutes. I noted things to her, describing how the paint looked, touching it in places (which she did not like me to do), pointing to areas I thought could have been done better.

"We want to put some small steps along the bottom; down around here, I think," she said. I did not know how many steps there should be, nor how big; neither did she.

"What if I check the other one?" I said, referring to the Patio painting hanging in the adjacent room. She agreed.

I counted twelve steps of roughly uniform size. I knelt in front of the new canvas, figuring out the spacing along the bottom so that twelve would fit. "Shall I place them about the same distance from the bottom?" I showed her with the yardstick where that would be. That seemed fine to her. "Do you want twelve steps here, too?"

"Oh, let's put in one more. It won't be the same then." Her reply had a playful edge, almost mischievous. "What would the art critics make of that?" I asked her, reminding her of the thesis I had read to her that she had found so detestable. O'Keeffe and I marked off the spaces. The thirteenth square looked a little stunted, since I had had to alter some of the other steps to make room for it. Finally, she decided to leave it off. (The week after completing The Patio I took careful measurements of the painting. The original sheet is included in Appendix A.)

The squares were painted in colors complementary to the ones above, yet more subdued, less brilliant—almost a diffused, flat, peach-toned red. I was not as fond of these tones, but, as more and more spaces were painted, I saw how they fit in with the composition. I had to use smaller brushes now, and painting was time-consuming. I found it impossible to use the finishing brush in such a small space—I could only use it for the center of the steps, and then had to switch to a smaller one, not designed for the purpose. Everything seemed cramped at the bottom of the canvas, and I spent much of the time on the floor, twisting my body to get at the steps, painting alternately with both hands, often taking breaks to stand or stretch my legs.

The day was exceedingly long, and the concentration on details exhausting, primarily because there was no natural pause in the work, given the size of each square and the fact that I was doing one after another. The demands of painting such small areas underscored again the newness of the activity and its difficulties for me. O'Keeffe left me to finish the work. Besides lunch and a short afternoon break, I worked steadily through the day. I mixed small amounts of paint for the squares, comparing the color freshly mixed on the palette with the ones already on the canvas. If I was uncertain about the match I asked her to compare the two. Every time I stopped I wrapped the brush in a towel wetted with turpentine.

One morning, O'Keeffe and I were preparing to continue work on the Patio Door painting. The sun had not quite risen over the mesas behind the ranch house. A cool, gray shadow rested over the cliffs. Looking up, I was reminded of an odd visual phenomenon. If the sun was high overhead, and one looked at the rock edge against the bright and clear blue of the sky, it seemed as though there were a line between them. I told O'Keeffe of that perception, of trying to look at, or into, that line.

She looked away at nothing in particular, and then raised her eyes to mine.

"You should begin painting," she said, matter-of-factly.

I was caught off-guard by her statement, uncertain what she meant.

"So you think *I* should become a painter?" I paused. "Why should I begin painting?"

"Well, you can *see*, you know," she said, looking back at me. "You have 'eyes' and can *see* things."

I remember painting the last square. It was after six and the light was poor; we had painted hard all week, beginning on Monday, and it was now Friday. I did not break for dinner, not wanting to disrupt the day's momentum. Finishing this area at the bottom of the canvas was the most demanding work I had done. After every few strokes I had to clean the brush. If a line was not as sharp or clean as I wanted it, or if the paint had built up in a ridge between the pinkish-red squares and the brown, I scraped off the edge and applied a thinner, finer coat. Sometimes, if necessary, I touched up the ocher. It was this kind of constant attention to details that consumed the afternoon and was now taking up the last hours of the day. Finally, around half past seven, I spoke to O'Keeffe.

"I think we're done," I said.

I stood up and moved away from the easel. O'Keeffe came to my side. She looked silently for several long moments, her head and eyes moving around the canvas, walking close to the painting and then standing back. Then she beamed. I could tell she was as pleased and as tired as I was.

"Well, I think that looks just fine." She turned toward me, and paused, her eyes holding mine. "What do you think?"

"I think it looks wonderful." We stood quietly. I moved to get a different view of the painting, another sense of it.

"Are you ready to become a painter?" she asked.

"After one painting?"

"No," she laughed, "it would take a little more than that."

O'Keeffe looked at me steadily. She had spoken to me over the last two days about this "i-dea"—she pronounced the word with a special, separate emphasis on the "i"—she had that I should begin painting, an i-dea I found amusing at first, until I saw the seriousness in her persistence.

"Well," she continued, "now you'll know what to do when you start your own painting. Don't you think you'd like to try one?"

"Are you serious? Me start painting? I wouldn't know what to do," I said.

"You don't have to know how to do anything. You just start painting what you see in your head. That's enough. That's all there is to know." Her smile was inscrutable across closed lips.

"But, you see," I began, "I'd start on something and figure out that I was leaving something else out, like it was unbalanced, or whatever. I wouldn't be *proper.*"

"Oh, my," she said with mild, dismissive emphasis. "Don't bother yourself about all that. Just start painting what you see. You'll never get anything done while you're worrying about what other people are thinking. You just have to decide that it doesn't mean anything." Her eyes held mine.

"I'd think about what you were saying, about how a good painting had small, middle, and large spaces," I continued.

"Yes," she said, "but you already know about all of that. Don't bother about what the art people are thinking, God bless them." These last words were emphasized by a hand gesture. "You *can't* paint for *them.*"

She paused for a moment and turned back to the canvas.

"Well, you'll know a fine lot about painting when we're done. Just look at how much you're learning." Her face swiveled to meet mine.

"I know, it's great," I said enthusiastically. "As long as I'm learning something."

We stood for a long while looking the canvas up and down.

"We'll have to see what it looks like in the morning," she remarked finally. The light was not good. The room was softened by warm shadows. I finally turned to clean the brushes and tools.

When I was done I went to find O'Keeffe. She was in a closet by her bedroom. I thanked her for asking me to help with this painting.

"I must give you something," she said, producing a small postcard, a photograph of a bust of her done in 1927 by Gaston Lachaise.[3] The bust was white against a black background. "Have you seen this?"

I had not. She did not seem particularly to like or dislike it. She sat down at the table and reached for a black felt-tipped pen that always lay in a white box or on white paper. She removed the cap. Squinting intently, she leaned close to the picture and, carefully, wrote her name across the bottom of the card, on the pedestal. She wrote almost perfectly. Somewhat unevenly, perhaps, but all the letters and script were contained within that tiny space. Turning the card over, she wrote her name again, adding the date: "8/20/76."

It was 8:30 when I left. Away from the sun the sky was turning black-blue. I asked O'Keeffe whether I could come in late the next morning—I had work to do at Juan's, and I also needed to rest.

A heady, satisfying mood gripped me as I drove home, my mood matched by the growing afterglow just following the sunset. It did not matter to me if anyone ever knew. At that moment, everything felt right to me. The world had never seemed so grand.

Yet it did matter that someone know, and on my drive home I stopped at Les and Jim's house to tell them. Their stunned response helped ground the swirl of feelings, from exhaustion to elation, coursing through me. None of us really knew what to say. Something more momentous than I had really appreciated had transpired that week. But I had been sequestered almost exclusively in O'Keeffe's world, and could not see its magnitude until I shared it with persons outside that world. I stayed not longer than an hour before returning home.

My journal for August 20th reads: "When I think of the gist of our conversations today I find that one thing that comes through over and over again is this: 'Do what you will, for your own good, for your own satisfaction—and leave other things as they be.' Often she seems to encourage one's whims or interesting wishes—that's not quite right . . . It's those things that are different from everyday pursuits."

In the Abiquiu house O'Keeffe had a separate room filled with books, essentially a small, though impressive, library. One afternoon she wanted me to look for something in there. I opened the heavy door and then a window at the other end of the small room. We walked

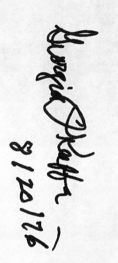

Gaston Lachaise, American, 1882-1935
Head of Georgia O'Keeffe, 1927
Alabaster on marble base
The Metropolitan Museum of Art
The Alfred Stieglitz Collection, 1949

PH 16-02 Printed in Western Germany

Postcard showing a bust of O'Keeffe done by Gaston Lachaise in 1927. O'Keeffe gave this card to the author on the day they finished The Patio. She signed the front of the card in the pedestal area, and autographed and dated the back. Use of the image courtesy of the Metropolitan Museum of Art.

around the room, admiring the books. There were hundreds of them. Occasionally she pointed with her cane at some subject area, or asked if I could locate a particular volume.

I noticed the wide variety of titles and subjects. There were many art books, covering painting, architecture, and photography, including pristine, reprinted copies of all the issues of Stieglitz's *Camera Work*. There were first editions of D. H. Lawrence and Mabel Dodge Lujan. There were many imported art books on Chinese and Asian art, all very big and expensive-looking. It was a fine room. When O'Keeffe wondered out loud what would happen to it, I suggested she give it to the Ghost Ranch, that perhaps they would build a special room for it.

She was interested in this possibility, and wondered whether they would be. I thought they would, and said I could check with someone there. Nothing ever came of the idea, though I did talk about it with Aubrey Owen, who worked for the Ghost Ranch Conference Center.

As the summer began to draw to an end O'Keeffe asked me, increasingly with concern in her voice, how I got along with Juan. It varied, I said: we had our ups and downs. When I asked her how she got along with him, she was very guarded, and would reply emphatically, "I won't talk about Juan," thus ending the conversation. I knew her loyalty in some way was to Hamilton, though later I came to question the notion of such loyalty. O'Keeffe would not argue or disagree with him in any respect. As she came to trust me she talked more about him, though always with reserve, and as if much was held back.

By this time (summer, 1976) O'Keeffe had known Hamilton for almost three years—they had met in the fall of 1973, some two years after she lost her central eyesight. During that time a complicated relationship and interdependency had developed between them, the specifics of which I could only guess at. It was not difficult for me to refrain from talking about Juan, since there was too much that was unknown to me. So I kept out of our conversations my deep misgivings about him and the misunderstandings I had had with him before.

Earlier that summer, when Hamilton returned to do the monthly payroll, I asked for several days off. Though I really needed the break, I also wanted to keep my distance from the two of them while they were together. I knew Hamilton was not pleased about my increasingly close relationship with O'Keeffe. On more than one occasion I had answered the phone for O'Keeffe when Hamilton happened to be calling from New York. I could hear his surprise, and then anger, that I was close enough to the phone, and, therefore, to O'Keeffe, to answer it for her. Full of suspicion, he would ask me what I was doing inside.

Hamilton returned only once over the summer, at the beginning of August. I picked him up at the airport in Albuquerque. I remember distinctly the last few hundred feet of road as we drove up to his house in Barranco. It was late, around midnight. He asked me how work had been going, how much work I was getting done on the trim, and whether O'Keeffe was asking me for help with "her things." I told him very little of the trim had been painted since I had been spending so much time with O'Keeffe. He asked me what I had been doing with her, and I told him. Suddenly he turned to me and exclaimed accusingly: "You've been eating with her, haven't you!" I felt the full force of his anger and jealousy in a way I never had before. For a moment I felt terrible, as if I had committed a wrong. I realized later how childish and cowardly my reaction was, for I had bowed to his judgment on an innocent and pleasurable relationship between O'Keeffe and myself.

The end of that afternoon in the library found us sitting along one of the walls. The light from the window illuminated warmly the books beside O'Keeffe, who faced me with the back of her shoulders angled toward the sun. I saw that her face was drawn and unusually pensive, lines of worry layered on ones of age. We had been sitting quietly. Her right hand rested on her cane. The room was still. Suddenly I noticed that O'Keeffe was looking intently at me. She spoke one short sentence.

"Oh, I *do* hope you and Juan can get along." Her words, uncharacteristically full of pathos, jarred me, and something lurched sickeningly inside. For a long moment she looked intensely, movingly, at me, her eyes steadily holding mine. A sense of uneasiness came over me. I did not know how to respond.

"I do too," I said, faltering.

In an instant, the reality of our relationship, its fragilities and contingencies, was alluded to, even if not discussed. I felt too strongly a sudden poignancy shared with O'Keeffe, as if the common verities upon which our relationship was built were as transient as the summer or the light fading from this room.

A Day with Juan

Completing the Patio painting was an exhilarating experience for me. Only a few members of O'Keeffe's staff knew about our collaboration, so the satisfaction I felt was largely private, and shared primarily with O'Keeffe. It was quite an accomplishment in my mind that O'Keeffe was so pleased with what she called "our painting." I was struck by the momentous nature of what had just transpired: I had painted with Georgia O'Keeffe, I repeated to myself, as though repetition would somehow fuse with reality the part of me that observed these events from afar in disbelief and wonder. I treasured this fact, fed on it, basked in it gratefully, and clung to it as a personal source of sustenance and validation.

The bond established with O'Keeffe in painting was manifested in subtle and direct ways. Conversation with her came easily; my comfort in her presence was nearly complete. O'Keeffe's attention to me in return was marked with a genuine interest in becoming more deeply acquainted, in wanting to know what I thought or had to say on all manner of things. So broad and unrestrained was the overall shift that I was constantly amazed at the swiftness of the changes; a few weeks earlier I could not have imagined their like, nor that I could adapt to them so quickly.

The days had been long; we had worked steadily and hard, caught in an internal momentum that kept our enthusiasm high until the work was completed. I found the newness of the activity demanded an extraordinary concentration. In seeking to maintain O'Keeffe's standards, I strived diligently to determine the skills necessary and to acquire them as perfectly as I was capable. O'Keeffe's casual and relaxed manner, which, as I have said, did much to attenuate the anxiety of painting with her, simultaneously accentuated my lack of training in this specific endeavor. Often I had to formulate "principles" that stated in a rough way my understanding of something O'Keeffe said—or, as likely, left unsaid—so that she could assent to, disagree with, or otherwise modify my understanding.

Lacking, initially at least, was the kind of feedback necessary for effective instruction. In large measure this was owing to O'Keeffe's loss of visual acuity. Until we devised an effective means for her to communicate skills that were for her second nature, I was often unsure if what I was doing was "correct." Though these stresses lessened toward the end of the Patio project, I felt strongly the absence of some sort of apprenticeship, and felt what little "training" I had was not giving me the kind of confidence that comes with continued practice.

The prospect of a completed painting, of seeing what this idea would look like, became irresistible to O'Keeffe in those first days. Daily, hourly, we watched the canvas take shape and saw the interaction of the colors. O'Keeffe's mood changed as more of the canvas was painted, growing in zest and lightheartedness. I remember painting the strip of cerulean blue and the quiet, but noticeable, excitement she took in it. Her face was brighter, her eyes less dim, her demeanor inwardly animated; it seemed the days held an interest and focus unlike that of the simple routine that prevailed before she again became engaged in painting.

O'Keeffe never wanted to linger too long in our breaks, and even shortened her afternoon rest so that we could resume painting sooner. She liked handling the brushes and the tubes of paint, liked putting on a painting apron and rolling up her sleeves. This was work at its best. Clearly, O'Keeffe was tied as much to the activity of painting as to the day's accomplishments. Her physical inability to paint was overridden by the obvious pleasure she took in a new relationship to painting, and in its tonic affirmation of a lifelong passion and commitment. Her spirit was lifted in a way I had not seen before, nor would ever see again. During those weeks, it seemed I was with a woman far younger and livelier than the one I had first met.

When I arrived each morning, I discovered O'Keeffe had already been studying the painting. "I've been up looking at our painting," she would say, and then follow with what she liked about it. She never changed the basic idea for the painting, yet what little we had done helped her clarify what she wanted to see in it.

The powerful effect that even a partially painted canvas had was remarkable. Each morning when I walked into the studio, a room simple in its greeting, I was surprised at how quickly and irresistibly my eye was drawn to the easel. The canvas had an unmistakable presence. Whatever was painted one day stood out the next with special force, the brightly lit white walls setting off the blues, browns, reds, and oranges. It was quite novel for me to experience the way my memory of the previous day's accomplishments in no way fitted the first viewing of the painting the following morning. The painting was more vibrant and alive, the pigments newer and fresher than the picture I had left with the night before. This contrast was striking, and more than once I remarked on it to O'Keeffe.

After we completed The Patio, I attempted to return to the outside painting, but it was useless. I would work an hour or so before O'Keeffe called me in to spend the day with her. How I looked forward to this time! There was more than enough to do directly for and with her. The only time I worked on the outside of the house was during her afternoon rest. Even then, as often as not, there was correspondence to be typed, so the house painting naturally ceased altogether. By this time, O'Keeffe and I were eating lunch together, and usually the evening meal as well.

Toward the end of August O'Keeffe began to show people "her painting," something she said with a twinkle in her eye when I was in the vicinity, and with an impenetrable look for everyone else. I was not supposed to say anything about my involvement with it. There was nothing intentionally duplicitous about her request. I had the clear sense that with sustained questioning on someone else's part she would reveal that she had had assistance. When several other people—Jean and Oliver Seth, I think, among them[1]—were invited to lunch at the ranch house, I moved The Patio into the dining room and hung it above the fireplace.[2] I joined the group for lunch. The guests admired the painting and were amazed that O'Keeffe was painting again. The satisfaction she took in their praise was obvious; I imagined that it was as much from our sharing a secret as it was from having one of her ideas realized in paint once again.

After Juan returned in September I hoped it might be possible for the three of us to coexist peacefully. There were, however, some immediate changes, following the break of several days I took upon Juan's return: the long hours I had spent daily with O'Keeffe, reading to her, taking down her replies to letters, or simply passing time in her company, were now a thing of the past. I no longer ate meals with her. She still asked me to assist her with small chores, and occasionally to read to her, but I felt a shift in my relationship with her which reflected Juan's presence.

Inwardly I felt uneasy. From what I knew of Juan, and from the few indications O'Keeffe gave me of his importance in her affairs, I sensed how my hope for continuing a close relationship with O'Keeffe was probably futile. He had already reacted angrily on the phone and in person to my daily contact with O'Keeffe. I had witnessed several blow-ups between Juan and others before, and had been on the receiving end of his temper myself. When O'Keeffe was present during these scenes, she stood by silently, withdrawn, her eyes slightly downcast, focusing distantly. Though Juan approved of the painting O'Keeffe and I had done, there was a reserve, a slight offense, even some jealousy, mixed in with his praise. When I took all these factors into account, it was hard for me to imagine Juan settling for anything less than occupying the central and sole role in O'Keeffe's life. Nor could I envision O'Keeffe standing up to him on this matter.

Still, I clung to the possibility that Juan and I might have complementary, not competing, roles in O'Keeffe's life. I was more than willing to acknowledge Juan's "seniority." In some conversations with him shortly after his return, I suggested how we might divide the work along lines that acknowledged our difference in status: I could continue helping O'Keeffe with her painting and with all of her correspondence (except for business-related matters), read to her, and so on, thus freeing Juan up for working with her on art-related affairs, exhibition possibilities, travel, and so forth. Juan's initially favorable response to my suggestions surprised me. However, the surprise actually accentuated the sense of unreality and foreboding in the back of my mind.

On the few occasions when O'Keeffe, Juan, and I were together—for example, when I was showing Juan which correspondence I had done and which I had left for him—I felt none of us was comfortable. We functioned better with each other on a one-on-one basis than when all three of us were present. Juan did not know how to accommodate my presence. O'Keeffe, in turn, seemed more reserved toward me and Juan, while I tried to act as personably to both as I would if I were alone with one or the other. Again, I thought, the awkwardness over time could be replaced by a working relationship established on trust and good faith.

After several days I returned to the ranch house and the long-neglected trim. It had been months since I had worked on it. Beginning the task again underscored the change in my status in O'Keeffe's world, a change that became more marked as the weeks went by. No longer did I have access to intimate, daily contact with O'Keeffe, and the events of the summer seemed almost unreal.

At first my work went fine, though I found the transition extraordinarily difficult. Nonetheless, I worked diligently. Increasingly, however, I sensed a strange, but not altogether unfamiliar, animosity on Juan's part. Every few days he came outside to monitor my work. Something was obviously bothering him, and soon his comments betrayed an irrational anger: it should not, he said, have taken me so long to paint the trim. Before I could reply, he turned abruptly and walked off. It took several moments for me to accept his complete disavowal of the time I had spent with O'Keeffe and the work I had done with her, all of which had been detailed for him in phone calls and upon his return. Often, I called out my replies to his back. I finally realized how absurd it was to try to convince him of what he obviously knew.

The tensions finally came to a head. I was working at the ranch house when Juan came out once again to "check" my work. He went immediately to some of the windows where the preparation had not been completed—they needed caulking and putty before a coat of white primer paint could be applied. Picking off rotten pieces of putty around the window, he said yet again that I should have been finished by now.

"I haven't gotten to that window yet," I said, as Juan looked it over.

"Well, John, I don't know what you've been doing all summer. We hired you to paint the trim on the house, and it's not done."

"No, it's not, because I was with O'Keeffe. You know that." I paused. "You said if she needed my help, I should drop the painting."

Juan walked along the house for a short distance.

"Some of this hasn't been done at all," he said, seemingly oblivious to what I had just said. His remark left me speechless. He continued reiterating that the work was not completed, while ignoring the conditions under which the work had been suspended. The situation was preposterous. As our "conversation" continued, we both grew angrier, though for different reasons.

Finally I said, "Let's ask Miss O'Keeffe." Juan turned, and I followed him through the kitchen to the studio.

O'Keeffe sat at the table to the left of the fireplace. I had not seen much of her for a couple of weeks, as she had spent more time over at the house in Abiquiu.

As he walked in ahead of me, I heard Juan repeating the bit about "incomplete work" before I entered the studio. He moved very close to O'Keeffe. I remained some distance away.

"Miss O'Keeffe, you know the reason why I wasn't painting the trim. I was with you!" I said, boldly and directly.

O'Keeffe was silent. Her hands rested on the table, her eyes lowered slightly, her sight off into space, not focused directly on anything. I was stunned. It was as though she were not in the room.

I continued unsteadily, shaken by the unreality of the situation. The longer I participated in this absurdity, the more it seemed to be substantiated. I should have realized immediately that I had put myself out on a limb, that she more than likely would not contradict or countermand Juan. Suspicion was being cast on everything I had done.

"Miss O'Keeffe, I wasn't cheating you. You know that. We . . ."

"John," Juan interrupted loudly, "we just can't have someone around who doesn't work. We can't use you anymore." Juan's flushed face wore a triumphant, unpleasant smile.

"Miss O'Keeffe . . ." I started, hardly knowing what else to say. I could not believe she would sit in my presence without saying a word! I felt anger and deep pain welling up inside.

"Is that how you feel, Miss O'Keeffe?" I asked, overwhelmed and resigned, still refusing to play the game Juan's way. Several moments passed while I waited. But O'Keeffe remained immobile, her expression glazed. She was not going to utter a word. I remembered then her words about not crossing Juan.

The odd smile still played on Juan's face. Suddenly, as though I no longer existed, he began talking loudly to O'Keeffe about something on the table, in an ingratiating, sing-song voice. Trembling, and without saying a word, I left the room, my eyes brimming with tears.

I put the lids on the paint cans, picked up the tools and placed them in the garage, and left immediately.

I found no consolation in the following weeks for what had happened. I hiked for many days, trying to understand O'Keeffe's dumb silence. I felt as if something had been wrenched out of my chest, something fine and wonderful that I thought could never be touched. I realized there was nothing unexpected in Juan's behavior—like an animal protecting his territory, he acted in the only way he knew how. I felt I was a fool for believing that things could be different at O'Keeffe's after the summer. "How could you think otherwise?" I repeated to myself over and over again. But the repetition did nothing to assuage the pain I felt, or diminish the anger at being treated unjustly by both of them.

Part of me welcomed the complete break with the O'Keeffe household. After Juan's return, everyone—me included—had had to walk more gently, speak more carefully, consider everything said and done. I ultimately refused to play the game his way, recognizing only later that what he had done had probably worked for him on numerous other occasions, including ones with O'Keeffe. But for me, release from Juan's tyranny was purchased with great pain. Much later, I realized that the woman I came to know so briefly was someone altogether different from the one I encountered after Juan's return. The totality of the change in her showed how much she had had to withdraw herself from the common decencies of everyday human relations in order to accommodate her relationship to Hamilton.

In the fall of 1976 Juan stopped by my house in Barranco. We had not spoken since the falling-out many weeks earlier. In the interim I had heard that he and O'Keeffe had traveled to the east, stopping in Washington, D.C.

Juan totally surprised me by asking if I would paint again with O'Keeffe. She had a new idea from their trip, and wanted me to assist her. Juan said I would be paid $5 an hour to help her as a "studio assistant." He did not know how long the job would last; O'Keeffe had several paintings in mind. I was eager to work with her again, especially in this narrower, more defined capacity, though I feared how different the dynamics between us would be after the events of the past summer. I knew Juan's presence would not be a positive factor.

As it turned out, both O'Keeffe and Juan were aware of this. I told Juan it would be hard for me to work with O'Keeffe if his attitude toward me continued to be what it had been at the end of summer. He acknowledged this, but brushed it off quickly, saying that "things were different then." He averted his eyes momentarily, and it seemed we were again at an impasse. But he continued by saying that O'Keeffe and I would be alone. For the most part, Juan would stay in Abiquiu when we painted at the ranch, giving us the freedom to work away from disruptive tensions.

I was very nervous driving over to the ranch on the day O'Keeffe and I were to begin painting again. I did not know what to expect. I felt the pain of our last encounter, and the ache from her silence. The O'Keeffe I saw that first day was formally cordial and polite. Surprisingly, the mood of the previous summer was still palpable and evoked for me during that first meeting many warm memories. But I realized with a sinking feeling that something had changed: our recent friendship was something she would not, or could not, admit. She asked how I had been, what I had been doing; I asked her about her trip and about the proposed painting. She described her idea to me.

Our conversation showed how much was not to be spoken of. We spoke only of matters relevant to painting. I discerned a coolness in her gesture and tone of voice, an indication that certain exchanges, permissible over the summer, would now be considered inappropriate. But I would not have felt comfortable slipping into the easy banter and give-and-take of the summer; any sense of fondness was overshadowed by emotional undertones from our last upsetting encounter. That O'Keeffe seemed to have closed off part of herself was revealed, for example, by the absence of eye contact. Even the painting apron O'Keeffe had had Ida make for my birthday seemed like a gift from another time. I was there to paint, and that was all.

A selection of oil paints, accompanied by small, corresponding rectangular color samples, was arrayed on a table, their names written in large letters on slips of paper. The colors were various hues of blue. O'Keeffe examined closely the names and samples with a magnifying glass, asking me to read the names of colors while she held up a swatch. We consulted the chapter entitled "Pigment" in Doerner's *The Materials of the Artist*. I read to her the sections on titanium, zinc, and lead white; ultramarine, cobalt, and cerulean blue; and vine and ivory black.

A prepared canvas rested on the easel. The first thing I did that day was to prime the canvas. Once she had given me the task she disappeared, instead of staying to watch as she had in the summer. I put on the painting apron she'd given me and began thinning the lead white to the proper consistency. There was an undefined anticipation in preparing the canvas. I recalled the thrill of watching the Patio painting take shape. Something of that excitement was present even at this stage, so much so that my discomfort at seeing her again disappeared. I had no idea what she wanted to paint.

As I applied the primer coat, O'Keeffe attended to small things on the other side of the wall partially separating the studio from the room adjoining her bedroom. There was a closet next to her bedroom, and outside the bedroom in a large open area, a table straddled the space partitioned by the half-wall. It was used by O'Keeffe as a desk and general work surface. She was looking at things on this table, going through small boxes of pens and pencils, and attempting to look at letters and other written material with a large magnifying glass.

When I finished the primer coat, I called out to her. She came over to the main part of the studio, and asked if I thought it looked all right. For the rest of the morning I organized the paints and materials we were going to use, collecting the colors she specified. Her voice was cool, our exchanges tightly circumscribed.

I ate lunch alone in the studio, and left soon after.

After waiting several days to allow the primer coat to dry thoroughly, O'Keeffe instructed me in an activity that she and Jane Oseid, a young woman from the Ghost Ranch Conference Center who worked occasionally for O'Keeffe, had engaged in previously without much success. They had experimented with tying twine to two pairs of tacks stuck into the canvas: one pair on top, five or six inches from each side; another pair along the bottom, also towards the left and right sides of the canvas, but closer to the bottom corners than the top tacks were. Twine was tied between the tacks on the right side, and between those on the left. When the tacks were moved, the twine roughly blocked out a shape in the middle of the canvas.

"I thought we could use these tacks and twine to make a line here," she said, gesturing toward one side of the canvas. "I thought you could move them around until we found the right place. Then you could simply tie the twine in place."

"Do you want to draw a line along the twine?" I asked.

"Yes," she said, with particular emphasis. "I want to draw two charcoal lines, one down each side."

I moved to the back of the canvas, and cut the twine into a manageable length on one side. O'Keeffe experimented with a number of possibilities defining a large, center section on the canvas. Using the tacks proved laborious; they had to be repositioned each time she wanted to try another variation in their placement. I finally dispensed with them, and, instead, held the twine tightly with one hand in back, near the center of the canvas. With the other hand I was free to shift the top or bottom position.

O'Keeffe stood four or five feet away from the canvas. Sometimes she came up very close to it and touched the twine, reinforcing what for her was an unclear visual image at best. I moved the twine many times, and waited as she quietly considered its placement. I could not see her from where I stood at the back of the canvas.

"I think that will work just fine," she said finally. I knotted the twine tightly in back to keep it in position.

"Now, I want you to do the same thing on the other side."

I took a yardstick and measured off the distance from the top left edge of the canvas to where the twine rested, and marked off the same distance on the right side. I repeated the prior steps and tied the twine in back. The bottom was somewhat tricky; she wanted the twine to intersect exactly the center of each corner. A tack kept the twine in place.

The shape marked off was simple. Two long, triangular wedges framed a middle section, a large triangle with the top sliced off.

She bent close to the canvas, nearly touching it, then stood back, and eyed the whole canvas several times from top to bottom.

"Yes. I think we'll try that. Now, I want you to draw a line along the edge of the twine." She walked to the work table and found the box of charcoal, handing it to me. "Pick one you like and try it."

I tried to draw along the twine, but found it did not offer enough resistance to guide the charcoal.

"I think it might work better to make some marks along the twine, and then draw a line using a yardstick," I suggested. As I did, O'Keeffe reminded me not to press too hard with the charcoal. Somehow the faint black line was perceptible to her.

Once the lines were drawn she asked again for the twine. She wanted to create two long, thin wedges on either side of the middle section; the wedges should come to a point at the bottom of the canvas from a larger width at the top. I secured the bottom at the corner, and maneuvered the twine on top a short distance between the charcoal line I had drawn and the edge of the canvas.

"I don't think that's quite right. Can you move the twine up the sides a little?"

I took the tack out at the bottom corner, and, while the top was still held in place by another tack, slowly moved the twine from the bottom corner up the left side, stopping a few inches from the bottom to let her gauge its position. When she was satisfied, I marked the top and bottom and used the yardstick to draw a line on that side. I duplicated the measurements for the other side. The broad middle section (the triangle with the top cut off) was now flanked on each side by two long, descending, triangular-shaped wedges, one of which thinned finely and disappeared at the bottom of the canvas.

The canvas was ready for painting.

O'Keeffe wanted the top third of the middle section painted a dark gray. The paint was to come part way down the canvas, fade gradually to a light gray, and finally to a white. I blended a large amount of white with a tiny addition of vine black, then carefully added black until O'Keeffe, who stood by, stopped me. She selected a brush and, as with the Patio painting, attempted to paint.

She pushed and dabbed the brush into the paint on the palette and then pushed and dabbed the paint onto the canvas with a similar motion. Her technique combined pushing with a more conventional brushing motion, such as one would use to brush paint on walls or wood. She stood securely, feet farther apart than usual, left hand on hip. After a few minutes, she stopped and handed me the brush.

"We don't want the gray to come all the way down, only to here." She motioned with her hand to the bottom of the top third or so of the middle section. I started by pulling gray paint from the area where she had painted, because it was too thick and glossy. It took longer than I anticipated to paint the area she indicated; painting to the charcoal line was difficult. There, I switched to a smaller, flatter brush, carefully feathering a thin coat of paint to the charcoal line. Periodically I stopped to mix another batch of paint matching that on palette and canvas.

After lunch and her rest, we commenced again. She told me to mix a new batch of gray, now using just the tiniest dab of black to achieve a slightly off-white tone. I applied this paint to the line where the darker gray paint ended, and almost two-thirds of the way down the canvas. She wanted the two tones to ease into one another where they met towards the top. Right at the line where they met, I took a third brush, and, following her instructions, began to brush the top paint down into the lighter tone, and the paint below up into the darker gray area.

Initially, of course, the result looked messy, but I knew from the Patio painting how the rough surface and the inconsistencies in tones disappeared after shading with the larger finishing brush. I gently brushed the surface of the canvas where the two tones met. O'Keeffe cautioned me to use only the lightest stroke: I should hold the brush, she said, as if I held a feather in my hand. I stopped often, and took a cloth moistened with turpentine to remove any paint on the brush, wiping it repeatedly with another dry cloth prior to brushing the canvas. The transformation of an irregular surface into a finished, completed one gave me enormous satisfaction.

After I finished this first area, O'Keeffe wanted the painting left to sit as it was. She instructed me to save the second tone I had already mixed on the palette for the following day, so that we could paint the last strip of the middle section. In order to keep the paint wet enough to blend with the next tone to be painted below it, I scraped what remained of it onto another piece of glass and covered it tightly with clear plastic wrap.

It was late afternoon, time to clean up. O'Keeffe had taught me to be meticulous about cleaning her brushes. After a thorough cleaning in turpentine I washed the brushes in the kitchen sink with warm, soapy water, then gently patted them with paper towels and dry, clean cloths. They were then always placed back in the boxes, cans, or jars from which they had been removed. The brushes I preferred were kept separate from the others. The glass palette was scraped and wiped, palette knives wiped clean, and everything arranged neatly on the table for the next day's work.

The following morning I painted a strip of the last tone across the width of the center section. I painted just enough to have something to work with when it came time to blend it with the lighter shade to be applied below it. O'Keeffe warned me against applying wet paint over that which had dried from the day before.

The center wedge was completed at the bottom using a faint off-white. The tone I mixed was hardly distinguishable from white, but we both knew there was a dab of black contained within it. I painted the bottom third or so of the canvas, again painting up to the band just above it. With another brush the two tones were mingled; the finishing brush made the demarcation between the tones disappear, creating a pleasing transition from light to dark going from bottom to top of the canvas. However, the lines defining the right and left edges of the center shape were uneven. I noted this to O'Keeffe as I painted and attempted to correct it as best I could. I was displeased with the results, even though I followed O'Keeffe's suggestion to scrape off any especially protruding bulges. I worked carefully with a palette knife, removing small amounts of paint before repainting the line. When I finished there was some improvement, but the long lines remained uneven. I repeated this procedure with the application of each new tone.

On each side of the center wedge I painted two additional, primarily gray, bands, looking like long tapering strips, pointed at the bottom, and widening to several inches at the top. Complementing the tones in the middle section, though not with the same intensity, these thin wedges lightened towards the bottom. We repeated the same procedure as before in mixing the tones, except that we began with a much darker color that contrasted with the darkest, uppermost section in the middle of the canvas.

It was difficult to paint the wedges. Their length and slight width, running top to bottom, accentuated the straightness of the long line. As I painted the first wedge I became frustrated with my skill, and told O'Keeffe again that the line was irregular and wavy. She simply smiled, seemingly unconcerned, and said it would be all right. "Just do the best you can," she said.

The final result was undulating and uneven. I looked along the painted line from both top and bottom of the canvas and tried to correct the irregularities by scraping them off with a palette knife and re-painting a straighter edge. The task exceeded my capacities at that point, especially towards the bottom, where the strips came to a delicate, thin width. The strips lightened gradually, if less dramatically than the middle, and had to be shaded. Here, too, I felt unsuited to the task at hand.

The canvas dried for the better part of the next day while I assisted O'Keeffe with small chores around the house. Though the discomfort of our first meeting since summer receded in the process of working together, I did not venture into more personal topics of conversation. O'Keeffe's responses seemed intentionally restricted. Periods of silence accompanied our simple tasks: looking for painting supplies, finding a box in her closet, tending the fire, bringing in wood.

The day after we finished the tapering wedge, we painted the outermost sections on each side.

"I think we should add some blue to the sides." The blue, she said, should be quite dark at the top, lighter towards the bottom. On the worktable, tubes of blue paint in a variety of shades were laid out, the small, rectangular color samples nearby. O'Keeffe raised high these squares of hard paper, turning them slightly to catch the reflected light. Often she asked me if such-and-such a color was on the table. I would find the sample and hand it to her. After thoughtful examination, she settled on two colors to be mixed and applied at the top of the canvas.

The addition of the blue tone—a combination of white, cerulean blue, and cobalt blue—contrasted strikingly with the grays and whites already on the canvas. The canvas was suddenly alive. O'Keeffe responded warmly, but with restrained enthusiasm, when I told her how wonderful and exciting it was that so little color could do so much. The blue was to shift gradually to lighter values toward the bottom of the painting. We shaded not only from top to bottom, but very slightly from the area near the center section to the edge of the canvas.

I painted the top two sections on each side more than once, for O'Keeffe was not satisfied with the position of the darker blue with respect to the darker grays. We experimented with different shades near the top. Sometimes I painted one color variation, only to find that she did not think that it "fit" right, or that it did not come down the canvas far enough. Other times, to achieve the darker color she wanted, instead of scraping off all the paint, I added the darker tone directly to wet paint on the canvas, going over it with the finishing brush until it blended in with the color below.

As she had before, O'Keeffe stood or sat several feet from where I worked, usually watching me, but sometimes, if she sat, she closed her eyes, her hands folded on her lap. On some sections, like the large gray-white center of the painting, I worked for thirty to forty-five minutes, applying paint evenly, mixing up more as I went, smoothing sections of it with the large brush, all without consultation, until I had completed enough to show and describe to her.

At the end of five days we had a nearly completed canvas, but I still did not have any idea what we were painting. As we progressed in our work, O'Keeffe asked me regularly, with a twinkle in her eye, what I thought it was. In a conversation Juan had mentioned it was an abstraction of the Washington Monument. When I told her that Juan had clued me in, she smiled, and began to tell me about it. She was struck by the shape of the Washington Monument as it rose away from her. Up and up it went, she said, leaning her head far back, a hand raised overhead.

Two weeks later, even after finishing another variation on this idea, O'Keeffe had yet to settle on a title for the paintings. I remember Juan walking around the studio and saying in a self-pleased way that perhaps something like "A Day with Juan" would be more appropriate than a title with the words "Washington Monument" in it. O'Keeffe seemed to resist the idea, but, when pushed by Juan, said nothing.

Gratifying to me while we worked that fall were O'Keeffe's requests for my thoughts and opinions on the work. Did I think a color should be lighter or darker? Perhaps it did not come down far enough, or came down too far: what would I do? I felt at a loss as to what to base my responses on. My remarks about likes and dislikes, about some colors seeming heavier than others, sounded crude and unsophisticated to me. But I was surprised at O'Keeffe's receptive attitude, and her genuine interest alleviated my awkwardness and discomfort.

In retrospect, I see there was something else that helped me communicate with O'Keeffe, best explained this way: O'Keeffe welcomed and was even refreshed by the kind of primitivity that characterized my responses. Her own manner of speaking about painting, far richer and more subtle than mine, was cast, as it were, in the vernacular: for example, her language described what she saw, or how some blues were incompatible with others, or how she wanted to give the feeling in the Washington Monument painting of something rising away from and towering over the viewer. But, although she preferred to speak simply and directly about her craft, what she had to say was no less accurate or insightful because of its simplicity than the obscure and self-indulgent character of aesthetic reflection by other artists.

The directness of her approach made O'Keeffe simultaneously more accessible and more imposing to me than if she had spoken the most theory-laden language imaginable. She seemed to say more with a few words and a gesture than others who chose to speak paragraphs about the same matters. It was clear to me that nothing in the way of understanding was sacrificed in her remarks: simplicity, I discovered, need not be simplistic. The casual, piecemeal introduction over the summer to her daily life and way of thinking; the easy companionship that led to painting The Patio; even the time away from her world gave me some sense of how she saw and appreciated things.

My suggestions were not always appropriate. On the first Monument painting, O'Keeffe was initially dissatisfied with the value of the blue near the top. I suggested—and she agreed to try, even though she felt the color was wrong—the addition of a little ultramarine. I mixed some ultramarine with a portion of the blue shade we were using, and applied it to the top of the canvas on both sides, after scraping off the other color. I shaded a small section on both sides, and we stood back.

"No, that won't do," O'Keeffe said after a short pause. "It's not right. The blue is different. You better scrape it off." (Some of the ultramarine still stands out in the photograph of the painting reproduced in *ARTnews* magazine.)

O'Keeffe experimented in the second Monument painting with an idea of her own. She thought some green should be added towards the bottom of the outside wedges, where the blue was coming down. I mixed up the colors she suggested and applied it. I had hardly finished doing so when she said, simply, "It's not right," and had me scrape it off.

The second in the series of what finally came to be called *From a Day with Juan* I painted almost entirely on my own. (I did not know the final titling of the paintings until I saw the first one reproduced in *ARTnews* magazine.) O'Keeffe provided the composition and the colors to be used while I strove to realize her ideas within the range of my capacities. The essential idea of the first one was preserved and simplified. Missing were the long, gray wedges on the sides of the center; the darker gray and gray-black tones were lightened considerably, as were the blues on the outside. The canvas was smaller, and rotated, so that its width was greater than its height.

More so than at any prior time, O'Keeffe left me alone while I worked on this canvas, effectively granting me more autonomy by her physical absence from the studio. Whether correct or not, I interpreted this as a sign of her tacit confidence in my abilities, and hence as advance approbation for whatever level of refinement I brought to the things I had been learning in her company. Though I still consulted with her (for example, on the placement of a color vis-à-vis other colors in the painting), the consultation usually took place after I had already mixed and applied the color in question.

This license to exercise and perfect my blossoming skills engendered a dramatic, qualitative shift in how I approached painting. My earlier successes in performing quite simple tasks (I had no illusions about their simplicity) were now coupled with greater freedom to improve upon them. Patience, exactness, and painstaking attention to detail were fed and nurtured by my new-found enthusiasm. I took great care in painting straight lines, in applying even and consistent coats of paint, and in shading as perfectly as possible one tone into another. In comparison with the first Monument painting, the second one displayed a higher degree of refinement and polish.

O'Keeffe was very pleased with the completed canvas. Much of the refinement I had been able to achieve undoubtedly escaped her weakened eye. But I described in great detail to her every feature of the painting: how the surface of the canvas reflected light, how the paint was applied more evenly on this third painting than the previous two (The Patio and the first Monument painting), how the colors seemed warmer and less brooding than in the first Monument painting. Of course, she scrutinized everything I did, whether a few inches from the canvas, or standing back at the end of the room with a pair of binoculars. These things, coupled with my enthusiasm and growing confidence in my ability to use the basic techniques she had taught me, did much to help her "see," and feel satisfied with, the finished painting.

A few months later Juan hung this painting in his house, in the large back room facing the mesas behind Barranco. I was startled when he remarked on how well it had been painted. On a ride to the Abiquiu Dam in his truck with Jim Kempes, Juan turned to me and said that a person could do very well in painting by specializing in the "simple, monochromatic paintings" of the kind I had done with O'Keeffe. I was surprised at his remark. It was not characteristic of him to say something like that, nor did it fit the history of my relationship with him and O'Keeffe. His words created a tension within me: the pleasure I felt in having my work acknowledged by him conflicted with the anger and hurt left over from the scene in O'Keeffe's studio at the end of the summer. He knew O'Keeffe had not painted anything on the second Monument painting, and he was encouraging me to continue on in some way. I felt deeply gratified with even this small approval on his part.

My association with O'Keeffe was invariably polite and comfortable throughout the period we worked on the Monument paintings. It never approached the warmth, closeness, and freedom of the summer. I was especially reminded of the changed situation on the few occasions when Juan came to the ranch house while we were painting. In his presence, the character of O'Keeffe's responses towards me changed. She became quieter and more distant, as though detached from her surroundings. I imitated her, not wanting to appear too at ease with her.

Of course O'Keeffe and I no longer shared meals. I brought a sack lunch, and either ate outside, if it was warm enough, or sat in the studio by the fireplace. Alone and working, we chatted easily, but certain areas were off limits. Any references to the past summer seemed inappropriate. O'Keeffe laughed less readily; her smiles were infrequent; the warmth she had exuded in the past when I talked about my interests and activities was not forthcoming. I did not feel free to ask her questions about her likes and dislikes. I gleaned quickly from her stance the clear, though unstated, refusal on her part to initiate or follow up on discussions pertaining to our relationship, past or future. I did not think any more of bringing in music or books to show her. Yet for the moment, simply painting with O'Keeffe again was satisfying to me.

When we finished the last Monument painting, I was at a loss for what to do. There were no more paintings to work on immediately, yet I looked for a possible way to continue working for her. But increasingly I could not bear the idea of returning to the status of a hired hand that I had occupied at the beginning, as if nothing had transpired since that time.

On a Sunday morning I came to the ranch house, thinking O'Keeffe and I would stretch and ready another canvas for painting. Even though O'Keeffe was not planning to begin anything soon, she had indicated she wanted to prepare a canvas. Jane Oseid was working at the ranch that weekend. When I arrived, I discovered O'Keeffe had something else in mind. She was irritable that morning, and did not want to do anything associated with painting. She seemed already angry with me before I arrived, and, in what was perhaps a childish reaction to her mood, I became irritable in return.

There was nothing for me to do, she said, but to move some wood from the patio into her studio. The tone of her voice was unusually sharp and dictatorial. She seemed indifferent to me; her remarks were issued in my general direction, but nothing more. Her mood was disconcerting; there was again some kind of barrier between us, blocking off any possibility of closeness. She had never treated me the way she was treating me now, and I finally realized that we had reached a point of no return.

I reminded her somewhat sharply that I had been hired only to paint with her, and that I had told Juan that was all I wanted to do. For a moment the color in her face flared up. She became visibly, almost violently, angry. She quieted just as suddenly, and gained control of herself.

"Well, then, you'd better go," she said sternly.

I remember distinctly facing the option of giving in or leaving. If I continued working for O'Keeffe, I would always have to defer to Juan and his emotional instability, being careful not to threaten him in any way; I would also have to reconcile myself to the unpredictability of her moods and the accommodations and concessions she made to him.

"Well," I said, just as angrily, "then I'll go."

O'Keeffe said nothing. She turned away from me and entered the studio, closing the door behind her.

I never worked for O'Keeffe after that fall. I saw her again only once, several years later, in the early part of 1980.

Through the Gate

In December of 1977 a cover story on O'Keeffe, entitled "A Day with Georgia O'Keeffe," appeared in *ARTnews* magazine.[1] One of the illustrations included in the article was a color photograph of the first Washington Monument painting we had done together. The title given for the painting was "From a Day with Juan No. III." I found the "No. III" both puzzling and misleading, since this was the first of the *Day* paintings ever done by O'Keeffe. I expected that the article would explain this inconsistency, but nothing was mentioned in it about this, nor about the assistance O'Keeffe required to execute the painting, nor about the fact that there were more than one in the *Day with Juan* series.

In the article, Juan Hamilton made a vague allusion to artists who were encouraging O'Keeffe to do anything in order to paint, even masking off areas to effect a straight line, something that O'Keeffe and I had never done. The article conveyed a disingenuous picture of *how* O'Keeffe, whose loss of eyesight was public knowledge, was able suddenly to begin painting again. Part of me was not surprised that information was withheld; yet I was certain O'Keeffe, under different circumstances, would have been indifferent to a public revelation of the assistance I had given her.

I was deeply upset by what the article left unsaid. Essentially, it did not matter to me whether my name was mentioned; what did matter was the omission of several crucial facts. I thought that there should have been an avowal of O'Keeffe's inability, in this instance, to paint without assistance, and that, surely, a footnote or paragraph clarifying a collaboration was a necessary piece of information for an artist of her stature. It struck me that dealers, agents, museums, private owners, and the viewing public at large all would want to know which paintings O'Keeffe had executed by herself and which ones she had not. But more important was the simple matter of the truth. I reread the article, unwilling to believe it did not hint that O'Keeffe had required assistance, let alone that another person had executed her ideas, or that there had been any kind of collaboration.

The suppression of this information gnawed at me in the following months. If I did not say something about the paintings before O'Keeffe died, the truth would rest between Juan and me. Given the nature of our relationship and the difficulties between us, I knew he would do nothing to help verify what O'Keeffe and I had done. For a year and a half I remained in a quandary about the whole affair. No one but family and one or two close friends knew of my collaboration with O'Keeffe.

In the spring of 1980, my sister mentioned my predicament in general terms to a mutual friend and artist, James Harrill, who lived in Cañones, a village almost a half hour past Abiquiu. He was exceedingly interested in the story, and thought my concerns were legitimate. Shortly thereafter, I began talking to him directly about my work with O'Keeffe. Because he knew far more intimately than I the peculiar workings of the art world, we explored in conversation the permutations, real and imagined, of the situation. Above all, he supported my fundamental concern that the truth be known. After numerous conversations at his home, we decided the first step was to talk directly to O'Keeffe.

It took all my nerve to drive to O'Keeffe's Abiquiu house, climb out of the Volkswagen, and walk towards the house. A large, tall gate, consisting of a wood frame with large-mesh wire over it, the kind with five- or six-inch squares, blocked the entrance to the inner grounds of her home. One of the dogs was in the courtyard area. As if I were

O'Keeffe at the gate into the compound of her Abiquiu home. This was the gate through which the author spoke with both O'Keeffe and Juan Hamilton concerning his collaboration with the artist. Photograph © Todd Webb (b. 1905), Untitled (Gate of Abiquiu House), nd, gelatin silver photograph, Todd Webb Study Collection, Museum of Fine Arts, Museum of New Mexico, Gift of Mr. and Mrs. Todd Webb.

expected, O'Keeffe was leaving the studio. I noted instantly her tired and somewhat unsteady shuffle toward the main part of the house.

"Miss O'Keeffe?" I called out. She slowed, and stopped without turning her head, unsure she had heard anything. I called again more loudly. "Miss O'Keeffe!" This time she turned to face the gate, squinting in my direction.

"Who's there?" she called weakly.

"It's me, John Poling," I called back. She stood at least twenty feet away.

She paused for a moment and looked away, as if waiting for the name to register. She looked back in the direction of my voice.

"What is it you want?" she asked wearily.

"I wanted to talk to you about the painting in the magazine article." I shouted, enunciating every word. It felt unnatural to speak at this volume.

"Well, I don't know if I have any more painting for you to do. You'll have to talk to Juan about that. He might have some work for you. Come back when Juan's here. I can't do anything for you now," she said, and turned to go.

"No, I don't mean work." I fumbled for a moment. The words I had carefully prepared now seemed clumsy. "I want to talk about the painting we did together, the one printed in the *ARTnews* article."

She picked up visibly.

"Well, what about it?"

"There . . . there wasn't any mention made of the fact that you had some help with it. I thought somehow it should be made known that you had some assistance with the painting."

She had moved in my direction while I spoke. Suddenly, she became agitated at my words.

"Well, it's none of your business," she retorted sharply. "You're just after something for yourself, aren't you?"

Her suspicious response shocked me. She seemed to have immediately assumed a nefarious purpose in my approaching her. Far from breaking a trust, I felt I was preserving one between her and the truth. It was because of the esteem in which I held her, and because of my sense of duty, that we were having this conversation at all. My voice sounded unsteady in my own ears.

"No, that's not it at all. I just think the facts should be known. I think a letter should be sent to the magazine saying that you had some assistance on the painting, that's all. That information should be available with the paintings."

O'Keeffe was angry now. Even though she listened to everything I said, it was as if she were predisposed to understand my words in a way that had nothing whatsoever to do with the immediate context. I felt with despair that my attempt to have the facts acknowledged had never had a chance. O'Keeffe seemed to believe that I would take advantage of her reputation for personal gain.

She said crossly that all kinds of painters had assistants without ever making mention of it. Besides, they were her ideas—I could not have painted anything without them. I readily acknowledged that, but countered that she could not have realized her ideas without my help. It had been a collaboration.

But the conversation was at an end.

"I won't talk any more about it," she snapped. "You'll have to come back when Juan's here."

I was thoroughly shaken by the encounter with O'Keeffe. Perhaps she is right, I thought; perhaps it is none of my business. I could not, however, lose my sense that the issue should not be left unresolved. Given the difficulties now, what would it be like in several years, or after O'Keeffe died, to establish the facts? I feared that I had already waited too long since the publication of the article; that I had assumed there would always be time to document the fact of our collaboration. I did not mistrust O'Keeffe; she might be angry, but I *knew* her anger was misplaced. In other circumstances her attitude would have been different. Her responses were a product of suspicions she was not entirely responsible for.

I realized I needed to speak with Juan. A week following my conversation with O'Keeffe, I drove again to Abiquiu.

I approached the gate apprehensively. One of the day-workers was outside; I asked for Juan. After a few minutes Hamilton emerged from the studio and walked briskly towards the entrance.

Juan seemed in a hurry. He acted uninterested, as if the whole matter were insignificant. I reiterated my concerns to him. Again, the conversation took place through the gate.

"I don't know what you and O'Keeffe did together," Juan said officiously, referring to the times O'Keeffe and I painted in the studio at the ranch. To be sure, Juan was gone that summer, and he rarely made a showing at the ranch house during the fall when O'Keeffe and I were working. But his disavowal of any knowledge of our activity was less than credible. He knew exactly what went on: he had had conversations that fall with O'Keeffe and me about the painting, he had talked to us about titles for it, and he had told me how much he liked the one I painted that he later hung in his house. His response only confirmed my concerns.

He said more of the same *Day* series had been painted, remarking pointedly that all were "much better" than the first ones. Setting aside the possible question of who painted any additional canvases, I told him my concern was only to make the information readily and publicly available: Juan, as O'Keeffe's secretary, should inform *ARTnews* of the omission. When asked if the information was on file, he said it was; when I asked whether I could see it, however, he fidgeted and said it was not available for me to see. The best thing, he continued, was for me to state in a letter, "as calmly as possible," what it was I wanted. In addition, a letter would be filed in the Beinecke Library at Yale.[2]

I thought a letter in the Beinecke was a fine but insufficient idea. I told him I wanted to correct the incomplete, and potentially misleading, picture given by the article. Furthermore, I thought this information should be readily available. Juan was unwilling to do this. Finally, he said he was very busy and had more important things to do. A nest of ants had been discovered in O'Keeffe's bedroom and bathroom area, and the problem required his attention.

The meeting with Juan was not reassuring in any way.

Many conversations with my family followed, and many others with Jim Harrill, who again walked me through all the considerations I never would have thought of on my own. Jim and I had long conversations at his old adobe on the road to Cañones. Jim was unswerving in his support, once he had gotten to know me and had come to understand my concern. He was an accomplished, successful artist himself; his acrylic scenes of Greece and New Mexico were distinctive, sharp, and clean. Often he worked on a canvas on his back porch while we talked, a rumble of summer thunder underscoring our dialogue.

Jim's was a first-rate intelligence; he was acute, discerning, sensitive, ironic or sarcastic or satirical when needed, sensitive to pathos as well as intellectual subtleties. Jim was steeped in artistic and literary culture. He was well-read, and his music collection, primarily of classical music, was exceptional. He permitted me to vent and explore, testing my thoughts and feelings against and with him. He left every move and decision to me, even as he presented all the options. We consulted a lawyer regarding legal implications. Initially, however, it looked as though there were no avenue open to rectify the situation.

For several weeks nothing happened. Then, Jim said there was a new possibility involving a writer, Hope Aldrich, from *The Santa Fe Reporter,* a weekly newspaper. She wanted to find out more about the situation before committing herself. Her cautiousness fit well with my own attitude, and Jim arranged a meeting with her.

Hope and I first met for lunch at Jim's house. She was interested in exploring all aspects of the issues, and wanted us to hold several more conversations. If she were to write my story, she told me, she would insist on telling O'Keeffe's side as well. Nothing could have suited me better, since I felt the situation would speak for itself. Hope was extraordinarily careful in researching the story. I gave her as much detail and background as possible. She constantly checked and cross-checked information and verified details. Later, she interviewed O'Keeffe and Juan, and their accounts appeared alongside mine. A shorter article covered the perspective of museum directors and gallery owners concerning the public disclosure of artistic assistance and collaboration.

The paper came out on Thursday, July 31, 1980. I picked up twenty-five copies of the paper from the *Reporter* offices, and drove home. I remember the day was overcast and gray all the way from Santa Fe to Abiquiu. Particularly dark clouds hung over Abiquiu and Barranco. After I arrived home, an enormous storm broke over the whole area. Violent thunder and lightning continued for much of the afternoon. My sister said O'Keeffe must have seen the article about that time.

I received a number of letters afterwards, some supportive, some suspicious of my going public with the facts. A reporter for *Newsweek* magazine in Santa Fe was interested in talking further about the events. I met with him briefly to say the *Reporter* articles said all that needed to be said at that time. He submitted a short summary of the article for the August 18, 1980, "Newsmakers" section of *Newsweek,* quoting both O'Keeffe and me.

The whole affair was finally at an end.

A Note About the Paintings

The two articles by Hope Aldrich documenting my collaboration with O'Keeffe, "Art Assist: Where Is Credit Due?" and "Truth Vital, Experts Say," appeared in *The Santa Fe Reporter,* vol. 7, no. 6, Thurs., July 31, 1980, 5 and 14-15. They are reprinted here as Appendices B and C. Appendix D is a copy of the letter from Yale acknowledging the gift of the *Reporter* articles to their O'Keeffe materials. According to Hamilton, after my collaboration another four to six works in the series called *From a Day with*

Juan were completed by O'Keeffe with one or more assistants. Neither the nature of the assistance, nor the name or names of the assistants, has been documented.

Of the three paintings O'Keeffe and I collaborated on—The Patio (1976), and two from the series *From a Day with Juan* (both 1976)—one (*From a Day with Juan III,* 1977) was reproduced in color in the December 1977 issue of *ARTnews* magazine (p. 39). I learned the titling and numbering of the *From a Day with Juan* paintings in a letter dated September 24, 1986 from the law firm of Jones, Gallegos, Snead & Wertheim. The law firm was representing those members of O'Keeffe's family who were contesting two codicils to O'Keeffe's 1979 will, and I had agreed to cooperate with them in their case. When one of their leading lawyers asked if there was anything they could do for me in return, I asked for help in getting more details about the paintings in question. (For more information on the legal battle over O'Keeffe's will, see Roxana Robinson's *Georgia O'Keeffe: A Life,* pp. 551-559.)

In Aldrich's article, Hamilton stated that the second painting in the series *From a Day with Juan IV* (1977) was part of an exhibition that traveled to five other museums called *American Painting of the 1970s,* organized by the Albright-Knox Gallery in Buffalo, NY. (*American Painting of the 1970s.* Essay by Linda L. Cathcart. Catalog prepared by the Albright-Knox Art Gallery. Buffalo, NY: The Albright-Knox Art Gallery, 1978. Materials supplied by Michele Hanson, Assistant Librarian of the Gallery. Hereafter cited as Albright-Knox.) However, the painting reproduced in the exhibition catalog (Albright-Knox, p. 46) as *From a Day with Juan No. IV* is not the second *Day with Juan* painting I collaborated on with O'Keeffe. Neither the dimensions nor the painting style nor the composition match the painting I worked on. (For a fuller description of this painting, see Chapter V, "A Day With Juan.") According to Hamilton, the "main reason" this painting was included in the show was that "he and O'Keeffe found a very fine frame that fit the painting exactly."

Whichever painting it actually was, the letter from the Jones law firm cited the approximate market value of the *From a Day With Juan* paintings that I had collaborated on with O'Keeffe, as supplied to them by the O'Keeffe estate as part of legal proceedings concerning the settlement of her estate. In 1986, the two paintings were valued at from $200,000 to $250,000 each.

The location of the first painting I collaborated on with O'Keeffe, The Patio, is a mystery. In the Aldrich article O'Keeffe is quoted as saying that the painting had spoiled because of a technical problem, and had had to be destroyed. Hamilton later added that "the paint had buckled on the canvas." In the same letter of September 24, 1986 mentioned above, the representative of the law firm said that The Patio was not included as part of the estate inventory supplied by Hamilton to the law firm. More recently, in a letter dated May 27, 1997, a representative of the O'Keeffe Foundation stated that The Patio was never transferred to the O'Keeffe Foundation, and that the Foundation had no photographic documentation of the work. (Letter from the O'Keeffe Foundation to the author, May 27, 1997.)

All requests to print photographic reproductions of the paintings I collaborated on, including the painting reproduced in *ARTnews* magazine, have been denied by the O'Keeffe Foundation and its representatives. The reason given by the Foundation was that the only requests for reproductions they could honor were those intended for "educational and scholarly publications relating to Ms. O'Keeffe, her art, or fine art in general." (May 27, 1997 letter.) My request for permission to reprint the letter from the law firm of Jones, Gallegos, Snead & Wertheim containing the 1986 listing of the *From a Day with Juan* paintings, their estimated market value, and the statement about the location of The Patio, was also denied.

Epilogue: The Wideness and Wonder of the World

The miracles of nature.
> One might say: art *shows* us the miracles of nature. It is based on the *concept* of the miracles of nature. (The blossom, just opening out. What is *marvelous* about it?) We say: "Just look at it opening out!"[1]

I heard of O'Keeffe's death on Friday, March 7, 1986, a day after the fact. I was sitting in the refectory of Yale Divinity School with Steve Phelps, a close friend. He told me about it in the course of our conversation over lunch, almost as an aside. Steve knew of my association with her, assumed I already knew and that it would only be a matter of time before I brought it up.

I was stunned. I felt instantly a return of all the emotions from that time and after, felt her death fuse the petty but intractable conflicts with the youthful devotion and the friendship of a summer. Her passing became a bittersweet boundary. I did not want it to set and harden just yet; my emotions rebelled against that. As long as she had lived, a hope of some kind lived, too.

I can see with the same blurred eyes images from that day: the paper bag that carried my lunch, the half-eaten sandwich, my friend's face across the table full of the pain he saw in mine. I do not remember the weather nor most of what transpired the rest of that day, except that my wife brought from work a copy of *The New York Times* with the front page obituary notice by Edith Evans Asbury. My journal entry reads: "Georgia O'Keeffe died yesterday, March 6. She was 98 years old."

In many ways O'Keeffe's death made more urgent the clarification of just what it was I found so memorable from our brief time together, of what I acknowledged in the beginning of this book as a debt of gratitude. I began to think through O'Keeffe's remarks, whether made directly to me or gleaned from anything I could find that she said or wrote. Slowly there came into view an image of those artistic and passional ideals which disciplined and shaped O'Keeffe. Only a few of those ideals were clear to me that March day. But, over time, the connections between her deeds and the principles that gave purpose and structure to her life have become clearer. Precept and ideal, wish, love, wants and enthusiasms, course through O'Keeffe's life.

In an odd way, the controversy with O'Keeffe and Hamilton demonstrated her growing need for the security supplied by another, with its own special commitments.[2] Perhaps O'Keeffe sensed already the cost of aging, the waning of her artistic impulses, and how her needs were increasingly met in the services offered by Hamilton. Perhaps I already knew and accepted some of the tacit conditions of her relationship with him when we first met. Mrs. Annie Adams Fields (widow of James T. Fields of the publishing house Ticknor and Fields), a woman whose Boston home hosted many of the great artists of her day—Emerson, Arnold, Jewett, Homer, and Hawthorne, among others—said: "With a great gift we must be willing to bear greatly, because it has already greatly borne."[3] There is, after all, much in each of us that generally escapes full public disclosure, and which, if revealed in moments of anger, irritation, and fear, does not necessarily represent our highest emotional and spiritual ideals.

During the years following O'Keeffe's death I was preoccupied with articulating just what it was about her way of seeing, her way of talking about art, and her personality that made her such a formidable and determining influence for me. As I worked to discover the sensibilities that suffused her life and art, I was reminded of how formative deep enthusiasms are in shaping our view of the world.

O'Keeffe realized early on in her life that there was more to art than sheer technical expertise. In the fall of 1915 she recalled: "I first had the idea that what I had been taught was of little value to me except for the use of my materials as a language—charcoal, pencil, pen and ink, watercolor, pastel, and oil. I had become fluent with them when I was so young that they were simply another language that I handled easily. But what to say with them?"[4]

The suggestion that art is language is a striking one and cannot be developed here. Yet there is a way in which O'Keeffe utilized that language that can be summarized in this way: O'Keeffe never looked at the world, natural or man-made, with a cold or disinterested eye. Instead, she regarded it lovingly, with a kind of awe and an endless appreciation. She never ceased to marvel at the grandness of the world's mere existence, and her primitive responses to the world around her endured unabated into her last years.

We need seek no further than her letters, her work, and her choice of a place of residence to become aware of this. In that setting she best felt the thrill of the common, omnipresent, and for most of us, overlooked items and circumstances of daily experience. "Cady," she wrote in an undated letter to Cady Wells, a fellow painter and friend of many years, "I am in the beautiful country—our beautiful country—It is quite green—cloudy—and very cool—And Oh Cady—how I love it—it is really absurd in a way to just love country as I love this . . ."[5] A single bright evening star, the wind singing through trees, flowers and bones, a mountain with a road ribboning past, a New York cityscape, a red hill and blue sky—these and the exuberances of her abstract works testify to O'Keeffe's constant connectedness to the world around her. It is no devaluation of O'Keeffe's art to see how it transcribes and realizes a passion for the commonplace, born out of her sense that our world and everything in it is anything but ordinary.

It is this enthusiasm and love that modified and shaped O'Keeffe's aspirations, artistic and personal, even when these were not always attained, and that exceed the severely limiting notion of an ever-present sexuality permeating all of her work. Instead, O'Keeffe's art encourages us towards the threshold of a spiritual modification of the self, inviting us to enlarge and extend those very capacities which are integral to living a life fully.

I think O'Keeffe knew that the capacities which enable one to hear trees sing and to see common flowers as something startling were not arbitrary at all. To be able to see the grandeur and magnificence of the world, to see the starry heavens as glorious and majestic, was neither an accident nor a slip in rationality or consciousness. No, these responses and many others are appropriate, even demanded of us, and are themselves part of our shared experience of the world. O'Keeffe was appealing to what she thought were fundamental ways of understanding and responding to our world, especially the world of nature and how we see it, and the special if not unproblematic ways in which art intersects with and extends the world of our common experience.

In 1956, in a letter to Anita Pollitzer, O'Keeffe noted the following: "We probably all derive from something—with some it is more obvious than with others—so much so that we cannot escape a language of line that has been growing in meaning since the beginning of lines."[6]

O'Keeffe saw how artistic practice was interwoven with human existence. When she says "we probably all derive from something," she is not simply remarking on her artistic influences. What a person is is indebted both to widespread patterns of human action and reaction, and to one's growth within those patterns. O'Keeffe knew that art (the language of line) is never isolated from human life, and to speak of art as language means that there are regular, constant features to art and human existence. The greatness in art is a function of *what* the artist abstracts from our experience and *how* she fashions something new.

This is why statements about art are not only about one's own feelings; they are not simply a transcription of one's emotion. At its best, O'Keeffe's art reminds us that a flower or a skull can have symbolic power beyond the obvious; that they can be arranged and portrayed in such a way that they elicit deep emotion congruent with the rest of what we know about the world. Hence, we can see how art can figure in a kind of reawakening, revivifying, even re-education, of the sentiments and responses proper to and required of us. In appreciating art, we may often find our sentiments quickened in ways that affect what lies outside of art's domain.

Attending carefully and completely to one of O'Keeffe's flower paintings can elicit not only emotions brought forth in response to the artist's use of materials to depict a flower; such an appreciation can also remind the viewer of just how remarkable a flower is itself. One comes to a painting with an experience of flowers, and departs, perhaps, not only with an appreciation of painting, but also with a renewed appreciation of what a flower is. If that happens, then the line between "art" and "reality" is blurred in a welcome and permissible way. For now one's emotions and responses, though taking place in two different contexts (namely, the aesthetic one created by the painting, and the everyday one traded upon by the painting), have a kind of interrelation and mutual interdependency.

But how do we characterize such a transformation of what is usually viewed as "the commonplace?" The philosopher Ludwig Wittgenstein thought that a way of seeing was ingredient in an artistic point of view, that the way in which one conjugated the world around one was not just given by what one saw. How does one "see" the natural world? As something to be exploited or loved, marveled at or dismissed? O'Keeffe claimed that it was not nature as such that influenced her work, but rather how she saw nature.[7]

Her fundamental way of approaching the world with wonder must be at the root of understanding O'Keeffe's art. This approach enabled O'Keeffe to draw into the compass of art all manner of subjects, what she called her "inspirations," and to deal with them with consummate skill. This way of seeing the world and everything in it as a work of art was likened by Wittgenstein to seeing the world as created by God, which makes it "certainly worth contemplating."

"But only an artist," Wittgenstein went on to say, "can so represent an individual thing as to make it appear to us like a work of art."[8] To put it another way, a work of art forces us to take as a work of art the object we are contemplating, and for artist or viewer to miss this power of art is to miss something central to the practice of art. It is essential to us as appreciators of art to take the object before us as a work of art, as something to be contemplated, just as the artist, in her transforming appreciation of some individual thing, seeks to realize through her artistic skill a way of seeing ultimately realized in and by the painting. From two different, but complementary, perspectives, artist and viewer share the notion that the work of art is something worthy of contemplation, lovingly crafted on the one hand by the artist, lovingly received by the appreciator on the other.[9] With an artist like O'Keeffe, we hardly notice how we connect "graceful" with the arch of a pelvis bone, or "lovely" with a ram's head and the flower adjacent to it, or "fine" with a charcoal sketch of a bear's claw. O'Keeffe, through her artistry, worked hard to show us ways in which these objects and concepts are commensurate with each other.

Art makes that which is seen lovingly into an object worthy of our contemplation; concomitantly, to see something in the world in such an interested way is to see it artistically, as a work of art. In fact, this way of seeing is fundamental to the practice of art. Yet, we do not wonder at everything or take with awe the ridiculous; neither do we lavish love indiscriminately nor exalt the trivial. Of course, such concepts as wonder, awe, love, marvel and grandeur come heavily laden with cultural, artistic, moral, and religious significance well integrated into human life. Not everything fits art or is fitted by it, and a wide experience of art shows us the shifting lines of its purview and the nature of its integration into the rest of human life.

O'Keeffe thought an artistic way of seeing the world showed us something of its wideness and wonder. It could elicit once again those primitive responses of sheer wonder at the world; not primitive in the sense of crude and unreflective, but in the sense of proper and primary, as in the responses we share at large with other human beings. Art becomes another place where we can marvel at the things that make up the fabric of daily existence itself. The presentation in art of objects in felicitous, sensitive, generous, and careful ways occasions appropriate emotions and responses.

O'Keeffe would agree completely with Wittgenstein when he says we must learn to regard a picture not as a symbol but as the object itself (the man, landscape, and so on) depicted there.[10] When once asked what was "the meaning" of her art, O'Keeffe snapped in reply: "The meaning is there on the canvas. If you don't get it, that's too bad. I have nothing more to say than what I painted."[11] In talking about a painting of the patio door at her Abiquiu home, O'Keeffe reminded us that it was more than a representation of something familiar; it was, she insisted, a *painting*, first of all. "But it's a painting, you know. That's what I mean it to be seen as, not a door."[12] That is, we are not to see it as a painting of a particular door—the door off the patio of the Abiquiu house—for that already shapes and predisposes our response to the painting. When we take the painting as the object depicted, when we see how color, line, form, and composition are used, guided by the title, then, in most cases, the difficulties with the subject matter of a work of art will disappear. We must remember to see what is before us and prepare ourselves to be tutored in unexpected ways.

O'Keeffe brought to her art a passion and affection permitted, even required, by the world around us. Her art is like a selection from the world thus seen, a transformation and representation of those things that are her paintings. The conventional distinction between abstract and representational is one O'Keeffe thought highly dubious, since what matters is what the artist makes, and her dependence on a language of line and its deep connections with artistic practice and human experience.

This is in part how her abstractions could seem so startling, familiar, even life-like, while simultaneously new and unfamiliar. O'Keeffe's art made familiar and unfamiliar things worthy of our contemplation. Her success draws on sensibilities, knowledge, and experiences so fundamentally shared by human beings that we seldom need to remark on them. For example, in some of O'Keeffe's pencil works the shapes are as suggestive of the folds of flower petals as they are of skin or wind-smoothed sandstone.

In *From the Faraway Nearby* (1937) the viewer's eye is directed by antlers of uncommon extension, but on closer inspection, the viewer discovers antlers growing from places on the deer's skull where antlers never grow in reality. The skull and antlers are seemingly suspended somewhere over reddish hills against a pastel pink to light blue sky. The shapeliness of the antlers, their refined and undulating lines, smooth and gray, raise the viewer as they themselves rise from the skull itself suspended, rotated, against (or over) reddish hills. Here, both the juxtaposition of the familiar with the unfamiliar and O'Keeffe's toying with the viewer's point of reference (is he also suspended, or is he stationary?) work with the title. Soon something distant and new becomes resident in us as familiar items of our experience—red hills, pastel sky, deer skull with antlers, a feeling of space—are put to use by O'Keeffe. When these and other experiences occur for which words are impoverished pointers, we begin to grasp the remarkable achievement of the visual arts in their enhancement of the capacities we have for talking about each other and the world around us.

What is art *of* ? Consider the following: compare a painting of a flower, say a jack-in-the-pulpit, in a naturalist's field guide, with O'Keeffe's painting of the same flower. The paintings are *about* the same thing, namely, a jack-in-the-pulpit, but what they are *of* is quite different. The field guide exacts its own requirements: for example, felicity and accuracy in representation, an emotionally neutral use of color, line, lighting, background, scale, and composition. What one comes to recognize as characteristic of such illustrations is determined by the aims of a field guide, namely, to help identify and differentiate a range of botanical features.

These are not O'Keeffe's aims. O'Keeffe said no one took time to really look at flowers, and that by painting them big, maybe she could inspire someone to take the time to look. Magnified in scale, they became one's whole world. She knew, too, that it was not enough simply to enlarge them, as if size or detail in and of themselves would hold one's attention. Something else had to be shown. One does not mistake her jack-in-the-pulpit for another flower, yet there is no mistaking the glow and radiance, the feeling of inner vibrancy, that seems to surge within her compositions and animates them with an emotional undertone. Hers is not an exact representation, vein for vein, petal for petal, yet the viewer feels something deep and *correct* about a flower was depicted nonetheless. We see the technical artistry in the use of the painter's media which permits O'Keeffe to say what she wants.

This is the quality, the *of* character, that is so elusive and difficult to pin down. Great art shows us—at times, it reminds us, too—how *what* we are familiar with is shaped and transformed by *how* we see it. Even this is misleading, however, for it suggests there is a way of seeing that is itself neutral, pure, and unadulterated, which is not the case. Rather, what we see is dependent on long-standing human practice and custom, where words like "miraculous" and "wonderful" are firmly embedded. So, in asking "what is art *of*?", surely O'Keeffe and Wittgenstein are right in saying: art is of something like the miracle of the world that surrounds us. The technical accomplishments of the artist —for example, the feelings of depth and space; the conveying of emotion; the life-like, representational aspects of her work; the finish and refinement in composition and the use of paint—are required by such a way of seeing.

What could be more startling than a flower opening out? Or, on closer inspection, what could be more wonderful than seeing its lovely folds developed in careful, intimate array? If these things are instances of the miraculous, then art and life become deeply compatible in their shared embrace of the wonder of the world. In part, O'Keeffe sought to live and paint in a way that was accountable to the fragility and demands of such a world as this. I say "fragility" because of the unobserved dulling and loss of capacity to see wonder in the world around us.

Yet her art shows us something else, too. Early in her artistic life O'Keeffe recognized how necessary courage was for artistic endeavor and creation. Though she wondered where her moorings were, drawing and painting things she had never seen done by other artists, over time her art made legitimate what she chose for its subject matter.[13] O'Keeffe's art testifies to the risk she took in accepting her own ideas as worthy of artistic development and contemplation, thereby putting them on an equal footing with the artistic ideas of others she studied and imitated in the course of her artistic training.

As viewers familiar with her work we no longer find remarkable, perhaps, the world she created and sustained. The abstractions, still lifes, the pelvis bone series, the skulls and antlers, the riverbeds, the red hills of the Ghost Ranch, the flowers—we hardly credit her with the endless care and courage in creation that resulted in the body of works now associated with her name. This courage was not easily won. The price was paid by her life—its persistent strivings, its search for excellence in artistic technique, its pursuit of solitude, its sacrifices of many kinds.

O'Keeffe, by emphasizing the "common things," granted status to what most would have considered banal and trite. "The common" was used by her to remind us of what we had become: people so hungry for the extraordinary that we fail to see that we are surrounded by it, anesthetized and desensitized as we are by the extravagant, the sensational, the spurious; people who devalue in our seeing what we see, or worse, who never learn to see in the first place. "Art," O'Keeffe said in 1945, "is at a low ebb. I think it is the direction of our civilization. It's that what is considered important has nothing to do with art. What our civilization is interested in is how much money they can make out of it and how fast they can make it go."[14] In coming to see the world anew, her art reawakens us to richness, magnificence, and mystery, and becomes a springboard into the extraordinary.

What I saw of O'Keeffe, the core experiences and impressions sketched in this book, are something I've wanted to share. What O'Keeffe showed me is equally available to any person, namely, the possibility of developing deep aesthetic, emotional, and moral capacities. The remarkable works of art produced throughout her life show just how seriously she took the notion of "filling a space in a beautiful way."[15] O'Keeffe credits Alon Bement, one of her teachers at the University of Virginia, with introducing her to this idea in the summer of 1912. It was an idea, she wrote, "that seemed to be of use to everyone—whether you think about it or not . . . Where you have the windows and door in a house. How you address a letter or put on a stamp. What shoes you choose and how you comb your hair." An examination of her work clearly reveals how manifold are the realizations of "beautiful" her art makes available.

O'Keeffe's life itself becomes an example of the achievements a person is capable of when he or she does not live haphazardly, but bears down on life with attention and thoughtfulness. O'Keeffe noted as much to Anita Pollitzer, an old friend whose acquaintance she made as early as 1914. "I would say that I was always busy and interested in something—interest has more meaning to me than the idea of happiness."[16] Interests (the *what* or subject matter), governed by precept (the way in which one pursued one's interests), meant that all aspects of one's life could be attended to and harmonized, as it were, by the idea of "filling a space in a beautiful way." The books one reads, the music one listens to, the food one eats and how it is grown, one's clothing, and so on, are all to be judged by the same standard. Whatever it was, O'Keeffe said, consider it carefully and do it well.

But, finally, there is no interest without the activity that accompanies it. O'Keeffe's achievements as an artist are grounded in hard work, persistence, and years of apprenticeship and training. "I do not like the idea of happiness—it is too momentary."[17] Though the ends were different, she brought to both life and art a concern with integrity and excellence that was appropriate to each. The deep satisfactions with her life that surely were O'Keeffe's were not described by the concept "happiness." Instead, her success at living lay in the striving, the continued seeking, the risk-taking. O'Keeffe likened her own life to walking on a thin, knife-like edge, from which at any moment she could have fallen off. Yet, given the chance, she would do it all over again the same way.[18]

Many of us have access to O'Keeffe's paintings, watercolors, and other work through reproductions or museum collections; few were granted the opportunity to witness O'Keeffe's daily life. It is edifying for us as individuals to be reminded of how another's achievements began in a field of shared human possibility. It is part of the purpose of this work to preserve a reminder of the commonsense features of O'Keeffe's personality. The stereotype of the emotionally and morally vagrant artist does not fit her in any way.[19]

Yet, if we only admire, then we miss what inspires, which is the range of analogous possibilities for achievements within our work and lives, for making them as satisfying to ourselves as O'Keeffe's work and life were to her. The sources of inspiration are then finally within oneself. O'Keeffe, like other teachers, was an occasion either for the artistic experiences her art made possible, or for thinking "maybe I could do something like that myself."

In one of her most significant tributes to Alfred Stieglitz, O'Keeffe said he "gave a flight to the spirit and faith in their own way to more people—particularly young people—than anyone I have known."[20] She said this was the "highest and brightest" in him, what he realized in his own work and encouraged in herself and others, and why she was willing "to put up with what seemed to me a good deal of contradictory nonsense."[21] These ideals were O'Keeffe's ideals, too.

Many years after my summer with O'Keeffe, while pursuing graduate studies at Vanderbilt University, I became aware of the tremendous collection of art O'Keeffe donated to Fisk University after Stieglitz's death. More than one hundred works by Rodin, Dove, Hartley, Demuth, Stieglitz, O'Keeffe, Marin, Toulouse-Lautrec, works of African sculpture, and more, were given to Fisk in accordance with O'Keeffe's belief that major works of art should be made available to institutions which normally might not be able to acquire such pieces, and hence to individuals unlikely to visit artistic holdings in the major metropolitan centers.[22] But in her statement accompanying the gift is something that summarizes the highest and brightest in her:

> This part of the Stieglitz Collection goes to Fisk University with the hope that it may show that there are many ways of seeing and thinking, and possibly, through showing that there are many ways, give someone confidence in his own way, which may be different, whatever its direction.[23]

Notes

The Barranco Road

1. For a history of the Abiquiu and Ghost Ranch area, including a chapter on O'Keeffe's life there, see Lesley Poling-Kempes, *Valley of Shining Stone: The Story of Abiquiu* (Tucson: The University of Arizona Press, 1997).

2. Recounted in Roxana Robinson, *Georgia O'Keeffe: A Life* (New York: Harper & Row, 1989), p. 525. Hereafter cited as Robinson.

O'Keeffe and Her Houses

1. Readers interested in color photographs of O'Keeffe's homes can consult the following magazines: *Architectural Digest,* July 1981, vol. 38, no. 7 (*"Architectural Digest* Visits: Georgia O'Keeffe," 76 ff. Photography by Mary E. Nichols); *Architectural Digest*, December 1995, vol. 52, no. 12 (*"Architectural Digest* Revisits: Georgia O'Keeffe," 144 ff. Text by Hunter Drohojowska-Philp, photography by Mary E. Nichols); *New Mexico Magazine,* April 1996, vol. 74, no. 3 ("A Study in Solitude: The Home of Georgia O'Keeffe," 50 ff., by Tamar Stieber. Photography by Paul Hester and Lisa Hardaway); *ARTnews,* December 1977, vol. 76, no. 10 ("A Day with Georgia O'Keeffe," 37 ff., by Mary Lynn Kotz. Photography by Malcolm Varon).

Summer Days

1. Noted also in Barbara Buhler Lynes, *O'Keeffe, Stieglitz and the Critics, 1916-1929* (Chicago: The Univ. of Chicago Press, 1989). Note 1 to "Introduction," p. 319, in "Notes."

2. According to Lucy Bourker of the Santa Fe Opera, Thomson's opera actually premiered in New York in May, 1947 (Telephone call, Lucy Bourker, 8 June 1997).

3. Project HOPE (Health Opportunities for People Everywhere) was established in 1958 by President Dwight Eisenhower. The SS HOPE was launched in 1960 as the first non-military hospital ship, bringing sustainable health care only to those

countries inviting Project HOPE. Andrew A. Skolnick, "HOPE springs eternal for medical and health volunteers in 29 countries on 5 continents," *The Journal of the American Medical Association,* August 21, 1996, vol. 276, no. 7, p. 514.

The Patio

1. The book was Max Doerner's *The Materials of the Artist and their Use in Painting, with Notes on the Techniques of the Old Masters.* Trans. by Eugen Neuhaus. (New York: Harcourt, Brace & Co., 1934), pp. 68-69.

2. O'Keeffe began teaching in 1911 at the Chatham Episcopal Institute, in Chatham, Virginia, and taught regularly after that at such schools as the University of Virginia, Columbia College in South Carolina, and the West Texas State Normal School in Canyon, Texas, from which she resigned in 1918 to return to New York. June O'Keeffe Sebring remembers how her Aunt Georgia would take her, as a young girl, to the museums in New York City, especially to the collections of Asian art. "She would explain [the paintings] to me. She was always teaching; she liked teaching" (Telephone conversation, March 8, 1997).

3. *Head of Georgia O'Keeffe,* by Gaston Lachaise, American (1882-1935). Alabaster on marble base. The Metropolitan Museum of Art. The Alfred Stieglitz Collection, 1949.

A Day with Juan

1. Jean and Oliver Seth were long-time friends of O'Keeffe's. Jean was a local art dealer, and Oliver was a lawyer and federal judge. Oliver's father was O'Keeffe's lawyer when she purchased the Abiquiu and Ghost Ranch houses. Oliver witnessed O'Keeffe's 1979 will, but refused Hamilton's request to witness a second codicil to that will in 1984 (Robinson, 549).

2. O'Keeffe never called this painting by the title "The Patio." This title was, however, the one used by Hamilton and O'Keeffe as reported in 1980 by Hope Aldrich in "Art Assist: Where Is Credit Due?" (*Santa Fe Reporter,* 15), reprinted in Appendix C.

Through the Gate

1. Mary Lynn Kotz, "A Day with Georgia O'Keeffe," *ARTnews,* December 1977, vol. 76, no. 10, pp. 34-45. The photograph by Malcolm Varon of the first *From a Day with Juan* painting appears on 39. Again, the title given in the article, "From a Day with

Juan No. III," is misleading—this is the first painting in the series—and erroneous, since the painting was completed in the fall of 1976. The second painting O'Keeffe and I completed in the *Day with Juan* series appeared in a traveling exhibition organized by the Albright-Knox Art Gallery in Buffalo, N.Y. The catalog lists the O'Keeffe painting as *From a Day with Juan No. IV*, 48 × 36. Hamilton confirmed this as one of the three paintings I collaborated on with O'Keeffe in Aldrich, 15. (See Appendix C for reprint of article.)

2. In the fall of 1984 I had completed my first year of graduate studies in the Master of Divinity program at Yale Divinity School. I knew of the collection of materials at Yale's Beinecke Rare Book and Manuscript Library, but had never consulted them to see if any of the materials regarding my collaboration—letters or articles—were on file. Finally, in November, I consulted the files on O'Keeffe and Stieglitz. There was no copy of either the articles by Hope Aldrich in *The Santa Fe Reporter* or the December 1977 issue of *ARTnews* magazine, nor was there any other information on file concerning the collaboration. I had anticipated this and brought one of the original copies of the newspaper with me, which I submitted to the collection. See letter in Appendix D documenting this submission.

The Wideness and Wonder of the World

1. Ludwig Wittgenstein, *Culture and Value,* ed. by G. H. von Wright; trans. by Peter Winch (Chicago: University of Chicago Press, 1980), p. 56e.

2. "I might add that I miss the feeling of security you give me but I seem to manage to get along in my own casual fashion—" Letter to Juan Hamilton in *Georgia O'Keeffe: Art and Letters,* by Jack Cowart and Juan Hamilton. Letters selected and annotated by Sarah Greenough. (Boston: Little, Brown, and Co., for New York Graphic Society Books, 1987), p. 271.

3. Quoted by Willa Cather in "148 Charles Street" in *Not Under Forty* (New York: Alfred A. Knopf, 1936), p. 73.

4. In *Georgia O'Keeffe* (New York: Viking Press, 1976), unpaginated. Hereafter GOK.

5. Cowart, Hamilton, & Greenough, Letter #125, p. 273.

6. *Lovingly, Georgia: The Complete Correspondence of Georgia O'Keeffe and Anita Pollitzer.* Clive Giboire, ed. Introduction by Benita Eisler. (New York: Touchstone/Simon & Schuster, 1990). Letter of 17 January 1956, p. 305.

7. "*Question:* What do you feel has been the strongest influence on your work? *O'Keeffe:* Some people say nature—but the *way* you see nature depends on whatever has influenced your way of seeing." Interview with Katherine Kuh, in *The Artist's Voice* (New York: Harper, 1962), p. 189.

Notes

8. Wittgenstein, *Culture and Value,* p. 4e.

9. Abraham Walkowitz, an artist and colleague of Alfred Stieglitz, remarked on O'Keeffe's mastery of artistic technique upon seeing some of O'Keeffe's first charcoals with Alfred Stieglitz: "'Just see how the charcoal is put on the paper,' [which] confirmed Stieglitz's feeling." In Herbert J. Seligmann, *Alfred Stieglitz Talking* (New Haven: Yale University Press, 1966), p. 23.

10. Ludwig Wittgenstein, *Philosophical Investigations.* Translated by G. E. M. Anscombe. Third edition. (New York: Macmillan Co., 1958), p. 205e.

11. Edith Evans Asbury, "Silent Desert Still Charms O'Keeffe, Near 81," *New York Times,* 2 November 1968, p. 39.

12. *Newsweek,* 22 November 1976, p. 76.

13. See especially her letters to Anita Pollitzer.

14. Carol Taylor, "Miss O'Keeffe, Noted Artist, Is A Feminist" (*New York World Telegram,* Saturday, 31 March, 1935).

15. GOK, Pl. 11.

16. Giboire, p. 324.

17. Ibid.

18. Remarks by O'Keeffe in a film produced and directed by Perry Miller Adato entitled *Georgia O'Keeffe* (New York: WNET/13, Home Vision [distributor], 1977).

19. This was underscored for me in a conversation with June O'Keeffe Sebring, who noted the widespread stereotype of an artist: someone without moral moorings, personally unkempt, and laboring in an unkempt workspace. "[People who think that] never walked into my aunt's studio!" she said. "Everything was carefully picked up! It was all so meticulous" (Telephone conversation with June O'Keeffe Sebring, 8 March 1997).

20. Alfred Stieglitz, *Georgia O'Keeffe: A Portrait by Alfred Stieglitz.* Introduction by Georgia O'Keeffe (New York: Metropolitan Museum of Art, 1978).

21. Ibid.

22. Charles S. Johnson, "The Alfred Stieglitz Collection for Fisk University," in *Catalogue of the Alfred Stieglitz Collection for Fisk University* (Memphill Press, n.d.) unpaginated.

23. Ibid.

Appendix A

84 x 48"
blue: 3"
to square from top: 8"
square dimension: 40 x 32½"
    from side, each side: 22"
    from top: 8"
    from bottom: 7½"
small squares at bottom: 12 in all
    bottom of square, 3" from bottom of painting, 2" tall
    by 5¾/6" wide.

Reproduction of author's original notes detailing dimensions of The Patio. The canvas measured 84 by 48 inches. The strip of cerulean blue came down 3 inches from the top of the canvas and ran the full 84 inches in width. The top of the bright, reddish-orange square in the middle of the painting—the door—measured 8 inches from the top of the canvas, 7½ inches from the bottom of the canvas, and 22 inches from each side. The square itself measured 40 by 32½ inches, the 12 small "steps" began 3 inches above the bottom edge of the canvas. Each step measured roughly 5¾–6 inches wide by 2 inches tall, and they were more or less evenly spaced from left to right. For a fuller description of the painting see "The Patio" chapter.

Appendix B

From *The Santa Fe Reporter*, Thursday, July 31, 1980

Truth Vital, Experts Say

By Hope Aldrich
Publisher, *The Santa Fe Reporter*

Experts in the art field said last week that they thought artists such as Georgia O'Keeffe who develop physical handicaps in their later careers and use assistant painters to help produce their work should acknowledge the help to the public.

O'Keeffe, 92, who lost part of her eyesight about eight years ago, has indicated she is not willing to do this because, she says, the assistant's work had no artistic significance.

The experts, who included museum curators, art historians, dealers and appraisers, said the possibility of abuse to buyers of such works was too great to risk withholding the information. They said many renowned painters of the past, whose original works sell for high prices, have distinguished between their original pictures—painted entirely by their own hand—and works partly or wholly painted by others.

"Purchasers have a right to know what they are buying," Edgar P. Richardson, art historian, author and former curator of The Detroit Institute of Arts, said last week.

"As much as can be disclosed to the public is the best for us all," Robert Graham, an owner of the Graham Gallery, a New York City gallery, said. "There is nothing wrong with what she is doing, as long as it is known."

But prominent art historian George H. Hamilton disagreed, saying he thought O'Keeffe's position was a valid one. "She has a constitutional right to decide what is or is not her work," Hamilton, a former curator of the Sterling and Francine Clark Art Institute at Williams College, said last week. "If she releases a work as her work, it should be hung as her work."

O'Keeffe's general works are now selling at prices ranging from $15,000 to $300,000, Gerald Peters, a Santa Fe based art dealer, said. Her most admired paintings bring from $400,000 to $600,000 in private sales, other dealers said.

The issue of public acknowledgment came up this month when an Abiquiu resident, John Poling, disclosed that he had painted three canvases under O'Keeffe's direction in late 1976. The composition and colors used in the paintings were entirely O'Keeffe's, but the brushwork was his, Poling, a maintenance worker at the Ghost Ranch, told the Santa Fe Reporter. O'Keeffe has confirmed that Poling did the brushwork.

Poling, 27, made the disclosure after O'Keeffe rejected his suggestion that the fact of their collaboration be acknowledged to a magazine that had reproduced one of the paintings. One of them reportedly has also been exhibited in a traveling museum show.

O'Keeffe has dismissed Poling's contribution to her painting as merely mechanical assistance, and not worthy of note. "He was nothing but a tool . . . He had no thought, no part in the painting except that he could do what I told him to do," she said last week.

The art experts questioned by the Reporter all said they applauded O'Keeffe's desire to keep working, and said they saw nothing wrong with seeking assistance in areas where her poor sight restricted her.

"I think it's rather sporting of her, when she can't wield the brush but still has the ideas and colors in mind, to have the assistance of someone who can complete works for her," Laurence Sickman, former director of the William Rockhill Nelson Gallery of Art in Kansas City, said last week.

But most of the experts also said that the public must be informed about which work is totally original and which is a collaboration, in order to avoid exploitation.

The problem with O'Keeffe's silence on the subject, art dealers said, is that collaborations, or "school paintings" as they are often called, are usually worth less than half the value of total originals on today's market. Forrest Fenn, a Santa Fe dealer, estimated that an O'Keeffe collaboration would have only one-tenth the value of an original. Even if O'Keeffe designed the painting, he still would not call it hers, Fenn, owner of Fenn Galleries Ltd., said this week.

"You can be the designer of a painting, but you're not the artist if you didn't paint it," he said.

Dealers and art historians cited many examples of renowned painters who released "school paintings," such as Rembrandt, the 17th century Dutch master, and Charles Willson Peale, a late 18th century American portrait painter. A portrait by Peale's assistant is worth only one-fifth as much as an original Peale, a spokesman at Kennedy Galleries in New York City said.

Peter Paul Rubens, the renowned 16th century Flemish painter, made the distinction in his notes between his original works and his collaborations, Richardson said. In the notes, Rubens often wrote "Done entirely by my own hand." Madrid's Museo del Prado also notes the distinction in its catalog, Richardson said.

"It's really a serious matter whether or not a work is a collaboration," he said, adding that he would label the three O'Keeffes in question, "A Georgia O'Keeffe With Assistance." "A good dealer would do the same. A shady dealer would not," Richardson said.

Appendix B

However, Juan Hamilton, O'Keeffe's colleague and assistant, cited Rubens, Matisse, Michelangelo and many others as examples of artists who received substantial assistance in their work but did not always attach the information to the results. In his later years, Matisse, the French Impressionist, cut out paper designs from his sick bed, and others pasted them onto canvases and completed the work, yet the works are considered original Matisses, Hamilton said.

In a case such as the one involving O'Keeffe, where a nationally renowned artist does not wish to acknowledge a collaboration, an assistant is right in making the information public, Graham said.

"Someone has to stand up, or else it only runs into disaster," he said. "It is the public's business. In a way, O'Keeffe and her paintings are a public domain. I think the young man is correct to speak . . . The Beinecke Collection is a good place, but not enough. There needs to be some way the public can differentiate between her own paintings and the ones that are collaborations."

Juan Hamilton has said he will file a letter from Poling in O'Keeffe's files at the Beinecke Rare Book and Manuscript Library at Yale University.

Graham cited the case of Everett Shinn, a 20th century American painter, as an example of how abuses to the public can arise if documentation of each painting is not public information. He said that Shinn left several unfinished paintings at his death, that his son then sold them, and that they got into the hands of other artists who completed them and sold them as original Shinns. "The whole thing has become an absolute travesty," Graham said.

The experts disagreed about whether O'Keeffe's reputation would be hurt by the information that some of her very late works were collaborations. Richardson said he did not think so. "I don't think it would do her any harm," he said. Fenn said: "It will not affect her reputation whatsoever. Most people know she can hardly paint anymore."

But George Hamilton, the art historian who agreed with O'Keeffe's position, said he anticipated a different reaction, and believes the Poling disclosure should be withheld until after O'Keeffe's death.

"I have a feeling the public doesn't need to know everything," Hamilton said last week. "The (Poling) story could have very serious consequences. It could rock the underpinnings of O'Keeffe's life work.

"It's too bad that she doesn't want to recognize it (the assistance) now," Hamilton said. But, he added, she need not do so. "She has a constitutional right to decide what is or is not her work. There is nothing wrong with what she is doing. If she releases a work as her work, it should be hung as her work."

Hamilton conceded that abuses to buyers might occur, but he said he considered that possibility a secondary issue to O'Keeffe's right to decide the question. And he added that since the paintings were among her late work, they were "not of great significance" anyway compared with the main body of her paintings.

138

O'Keeffe's most important contribution, her originality, is not being lost, Hamilton said. "The authenticity of an original mind—that O'Keeffe has, and that has not been compromised," he said.

Dealers and art historians said that O'Keeffe's later work in the 1960s and '70s lack the powerful sense of color and design that mark her earlier works, such as those showing barns, flowers and desert scenes. "Her latest works have a blankness of execution," Richardson said.

Richardson and George Hamilton both noted that the 20th century art market is emphasizing originality as never before in the history of art. It is a peculiar trend that painters like O'Keeffe must contend with, they said. "Today's emphasis on absolute originality is reaching the absurd," Richardson said.

In earlier centuries, he said, there was far less concern over whether a work was hand-executed by a famous artist as long as it was the concept of the artist.

Many artists fail to understand the changed view on this point. Thomas Lee, curator of paintings at the Fine Arts Museum of San Francisco, said last week. "An artist's concept of himself or herself is completely different from how the public sees him," Lee said. "We—the public—like to associate a picture with an individual brush stroke. I suspect O'Keeffe doesn't see it that way."

Appendix C

From *The Santa Fe Reporter,* Thursday, July 31, 1980

Art Assist: Where is Credit Due?
O'Keeffe Refusal to Admit Aid Raises Questions in Art World

By Hope Aldrich
Publisher, *The Santa Fe Reporter*

Now in her 93rd year, Georgia O'Keeffe, the New Mexico artist renowned for her paintings of skulls, flowers and soft, folding, red mountains, has courageously continued to paint despite the almost-insurmountable obstacle of failing eyesight.

For some of the works she has done since blindness approached, she has used an assistant to help execute her creative concepts, following a practice that has been accepted for centuries. But her reluctance to publicly acknowledge that assistance has now created a situation that pits the views of the feisty nonagenarian against those of some of the most prominent members of the art world.

This month, the issue of public acknowledgment is being raised for the first time. It comes through the disclosure by a young Abiquiu resident that in 1976, while he was employed to paint the trim on O'Keeffe's summer house at Ghost Ranch near Abiquiu, he painted three canvases, including one that has appeared in a national art magazine, and one that reportedly was shown in a traveling museum exhibit. The man, John Poling, said he made the disclosure only after failing in attempts to persuade O'Keeffe to tell the story herself.

O'Keeffe said in an interview last week that she does not plan to acknowledge publicly that some of her paintings, though her own ideas, have been painted by the hands of others.

"I don't think it's anyone's business," the proud, alert woman said in the interview at Ghost Ranch. She said that none of the three paintings on which Poling worked had been sold or was on the market.

But experts in the art field said last week that they regretted her reluctance to acknowledge the collaboration to the public. Most said they thought such

140

acknowledgement would not hurt her worldwide reputation, but that its lack could make a difference of thousands of dollars if the paintings are offered for sale.

The experts argued that in the present art market, where great emphasis is placed on the absolute originality of each canvas, collaborations are valued at far less than products of the artist alone, and that potential private buyers and museums should be protected by making known as soon as possible the full history of each of O'Keeffe's works.

"Both for the story of her career, and the protection of possible purchasers, it would be a useful thing to make the collaboration public," Edgar P. Richardson, former curator of the Detroit Institute of Arts, said.

Richardson and other experts applauded O'Keeffe's decision to seek assistance so that she can keep painting despite her handicap. "It (collaboration) is a phenomenon that occurs over and over again in art," Richardson said. "It isn't a disgrace. Life is like that. I see nothing dishonest, as long as it is told."

Juan Hamilton, O'Keeffe's colleague and assistant, said during the interview with O'Keeffe that he has tried to document the collaboration. He said that earlier this summer, he urged Poling to write his story in a letter which would be filed with O'Keeffe's papers at Yale University's Beinecke Rare Book and Manuscript Library.

A spokeswoman at the library said most of the O'Keeffe documents are open with the permission of the curator. Almost all the people granted access to the collection have been scholars, she added.

O'Keeffe, whose most highly prized works, dealers said, sell for around $300,000 —occasionally as high as $600,000—was struck by partial blindness about 1972, and stopped painting for more than a year, Hamilton said. She tried to learn his art of pottery making, with its strong emphasis on touch rather than sight, but when it did not bring her as much satisfaction as painting, she turned once again to her canvases, he said.

The story of how she went on despite the handicap, continuing to express ideas that were vivid in her mind's eye, is a story on one hand of a proud and courageous artist, and on the other hand of a gentle friendship and dependence that grew up between an unknown maintenance man and a world-famous figure.

It is the continuing story of O'Keeffe's almost-superhuman independence and will to work—still another view of that pioneer figure who struck out west, leaving behind her eastern colleagues, who braved days and nights alone on the plains to paint her beloved adobe walls, colorful hills and withered trees.

But it is also a seldom-seen view of O'Keeffe, during one brief summer and fall. A view of gentleness, of dependence, infinite patience, of affection and of homey common things like laughter, chats in a summertime kitchen and "tooling" across the plains in a Volkswagen.

And finally, it is a story of the disintegration of that trust, of charges of manipulation, of a relationship destroyed by the realities of the outside world, of an art market that wants each canvas painted exclusively by the artist, even an artist in her 90s.

The story begins early in the summer of 1976, when O'Keeffe was living at her Ghost Ranch property, and Poling, a 23-year-old maintenance worker, was hired by Juan Hamilton to paint the trim on the ranchhouse. Poling, who lives in Barranco, near Abiquiu, had done construction work on Hamilton's own house in Barranco, and had helped build and pack crates for O'Keeffe's paintings.

At the time, Poling, the eldest son of David Poling, a Presbyterian minister in Albuquerque, was an amateur guitarist completing work on a degree at the University of New Mexico, earning money at occasional construction jobs. He had never painted pictures.

That summer, Hamilton was away in New York working on a retrospective book of O'Keeffe's work, and his absence left O'Keeffe without his customary help in reading mail and doing other jobs in the house. Soon, Poling said, he found himself being used to fill that gap.

As Poling recalls it:

"I was getting less and less painting done outside. She would send out one of the cooks, or sometimes she'd come out herself and get me . . . . I started reading to her, reading her mail, writing letters for her—she would dictate, and later I'd type them up, read them back.

"At first, I used to bring my own lunch. Pretty soon, I was having lunch with her. She'd take a rest right after lunch, so then I'd go back outside, and later, I'd type up some correspondence, or drive her into town."

One day, after several weeks, O'Keeffe showed Poling a canvas stretched up on the wall of her study. The canvas had been "primed" (painted white), but the white paint was too thick in some places and too thin in others, Poling recalled, and O'Keeffe asked him to repaint it.

That took perhaps a few hours, Poling said. Then O'Keeffe wanted him to sketch in charcoal a composition she had in mind: a favorite view of her Abiquiu patio with a central door dominating the canvas and a row of flagstones below, similar to a painting hanging in another room at the ranch, Poling said.

"We drew out the basic design in charcoal," he said. "I would hold a yardstick and move it around. She'd stand back." After Poling held the yardstick at an angle O'Keeffe liked, he drew in the shapes in charcoal, using the yardstick he said.

Poling said O'Keeffe never grew impatient with his inexperience. "She seemed so loose. She'd say, 'Oh, we'll start over here.' I kept checking the other painting to see how many [flagstone] squares there were in that one. But she said it didn't matter. She said we could add another one."

Poling said O'Keeffe would sometimes sit close to the canvas but at other times would stand at the back of the room and study the canvas through a pair of binoculars.

"Her vision was sort of blurring all over, but there were little holes in it where she could see through," he recalled.

After Poling drew in the shapes in charcoal, he said, he mixed up some ocher-colored paint, the color O'Keeffe planned for the background, and she tried to begin the painting herself, while he stood beside her. But the effort failed.

"She tried to put a little on herself," he recalled. "But you could just tell it wouldn't work. She'd get too much paint on the brush—a whole bunch of it would go on in one place. She'd ask, 'How does it look?' I'd say, 'It doesn't look even.' She'd try to bring the background up to the charcoal line, but she couldn't tell how close it was. She was asking me, 'How close is it?'

"It was as if she got tired. She said, 'I guess we'd better scrape it off. You'd better do it.'" Poling said he went on to finish the background, then to paint a blue stripe across the top and fill in the door in orange and red, the colors O'Keeffe selected.

"I got such a charge out of it," he said. "I loved the brilliant blue and how it looked with the orange. It was a lighter orange, fading into a powerful red. There was a lot of shading of colors. If you had to be working, it was a lot of fun."

O'Keeffe could not see the names on the paint tubes, so he read them to her, Poling said, and she could not see color samples on the glass palette they used, so he would paint large color spots on the canvas and she would approve or disapprove them.

Once they started work on the Patio painting, Poling said, they did little else until he had completed it about five days later. As recognition, he said, O'Keeffe signed her name on a little postcard, saying, "I should give you something." For his birthday, on Aug. 29, she had her cook sew him a painter's apron. Between work sessions, Poling said, they would sit in the kitchen chatting about all kinds of subjects, or he would drive her to town, or serve as her chauffeur when friends came and they went sightseeing.

For Poling, the impact of O'Keeffe's powerful and animated personality grew greater and greater.

"I had never painted before," he said in an interview at the kitchen table of his Barranco home. "I didn't know anything about her work before I came. My sister had only showed me a few photos of her pictures. So I didn't have any awe of her.

"And then to have this happen . . . ." Poling stopped, his dark blue eyes gazing back into his memories. His hand played absently with the handle of a coffee mug.

"There was nothing else I wanted to do," he said slowly. "I was more interested in spending time with her than anything else. It was just so neat to hang out with someone like that—to hear her laugh.

"One Sunday, some friend of hers was there and wanted to go out to the monastery (Christ in the Desert Monastery near Abiquiu). We took my Volkswagen bug. We tooled out there. She was laughing. I felt accepted. I felt really equal."

"Later, I remember saying to her the only thing I wanted to do was just painting with her." Poling stopped again, overcome by his feelings.

When Hamilton returned for a short visit, Poling said, he felt anxious. "I went to pick him up in Albuquerque. I felt guilty for having been that close to her. He was asking me more and more about what I'd been doing. Finally, he said, 'You've been eating with her, haven't you?'

"The second time he came back at the end of the summer, again there was a lot of tension. Georgia was sitting in the kitchen and I was in there talking to her as I usually did. Juan wanted to know why the painting on the house wasn't done. He got really angry. Later, he told me, 'We just don't need you anymore.'"

After that, O'Keeffe and Hamilton went to Washington, D.C., around Columbus Day in October, and took some walking tours that included the Washington Monument.

Apparently, the whitish obelisk rising against a blue sky stirred new ideas for a painting in O'Keeffe's mind. When she and Hamilton returned to Abiquiu, Poling was asked to come back, this time just to paint canvases. "Juan came down to Barranco and said, 'Georgia wants to do some more painting.' I was really glad to hear that."

This time the arrangement was different. Poling said he was hired only to paint, and was to be paid $5 an hour as a "studio assistant." "Juan told me that if anyone asked me what I was doing there, I was to say I was her studio assistant." An easel was set up facing a north window in O'Keeffe's work room.

This time, the two used a different procedure to outline O'Keeffe's new concept, Poling said. The concept was a rising shape, the full width of the canvas at its base and diminishing to about half the width of the canvas at the top.

"We tied twine to a tack and fastened it to the back of the canvas, and I'd move the twine around," Poling said. "We'd move it, sit with it, then move it again." O'Keeffe could see the line the dark twine cut across the canvas, and would motion to Poling when she liked the angle, Poling said. Then he marked it and drew it off on the yard-stick with charcoal.

The color was to be a darkening gray within the rising shape, against a blue background. Once Poling started on the gray, and had learned how to shade it, O'Keeffe would let him alone for most of the day, he said. "She would leave me for a long time on the gray. We consulted several times a day. She was usually at her desk (across the room) or dozing in a chair behind me. She'd sit and watch and fall asleep. If I was quiet, she might call out from across the room and ask if I was there."

O'Keeffe was particular about the blending of the colors, Poling recalled, and sometimes would correct him. "'The blue comes down too far,' she might say." On the third painting—with the same theme as the second—Poling said, they experimented with a new color. "We tried putting in green, but it didn't work. I probably repainted the blue several times."

Poling said he thought the last painting was the best. "That one came out wonderfully. It looked like it should. That one I was pretty much alone on," he said.

And then, abruptly, the interlude ended. Poling returned to jobs with bands, and later joined the maintenance staff at Ghost Ranch. The poignant memory of that strange and brief time with O'Keeffe lay buried deep within him.

Two years later, it was revived. It happened, Poling said, when he saw the December 1977 issue of *ARTnews,* a national art magazine, with a 10-page article on O'Keeffe that included a full-page photograph of the first gray and blue oil painting, entitled *From a Day with Juan.*

Poling said he was stunned that the article made no reference to the fact that the painting was a collaboration, and seemed to treat it as another painting executed just like her earlier works.

"I never expected they (the three paintings) would be grouped with her others," he said. "I couldn't believe these were that good that they were going to use them. I would think an expert could see the difference between her work and mine." Poling said that where the different colors of paint joined, his execution was more exact than O'Keeffe's work usually was, especially in the second gray and blue painting.

As another example, Poling pointed out that in the first gray and blue picture—the one that reportedly has been exhibited—some of his dark blue brush strokes did not blend with the lighter blue background, and would be untypical of O'Keeffe's style.

Still, Poling hesitated for over a year before speaking to anyone about the collaboration. "I was really confused. It was the power of seeing something in print. 'This is the way it should be,' I thought at first."

Poling said he never has felt that he contributed any ideas to the composition or color of the paintings—or that they were less than entirely O'Keeffe's idea. And he has sought no additional money for his work. Yet a feeling of "unease" gnawed at him, he said.

"Once this [the *ARTnews* article] is published and there is nothing mentioned about her having help, what other reason is there for thinking it will come out? Maybe from her perspective there is no reason to do anything about it. Yet with someone else painting, the work looks different from her own. It feels different. I felt the best thing is an acknowledgment, so no one is misled."

Poling spoke with his father and sister about the dilemma. Finally, during the first week of June, he went to O'Keeffe's Abiquiu house to raise the issue. There, he said, he spoke with her briefly through the gate.

The confrontation was a far cry from the warm relationship he remembered. "I was quite nervous," he recalled. "She seemed aggravated already. The dogs were barking. She came out of her studio and asked what I wanted. I said I wanted to talk about the paintings. I told her that the information I'd seen published was bothering me. She said, 'What do you want?'

"I said I thought the information (about the collaboration) should be available to go along with the paintings. I suggested sending a letter to *ARTnews.*

"She said lots of painters have had help and not made note of it. She said the ideas (in the paintings) were not my ideas, and I couldn't have painted without her ideas. I said she couldn't have put it across without my painting, and that there was a balance. She said, 'I can't do anything for you now.' She turned and walked away. She was pretty angry. She said to come back when Juan was there.

"I was really shaken up, that she was so angry." Poling continued, his words coming slowly again. "I was confused. I thought maybe she is right. Perhaps this is accepted. I certainly doubted how I was feeling."

Poling said he talked the problem over with an artist friend, who urged him to try talking with Juan. "About a week later, I went to talk to Juan. We had the same positions, on each side of the gate. It was the same catastrophe.

"Juan said, 'I don't know what went on in there between you and Georgia.' He said the series (of gray and blue paintings) had been continued, and other assistants had been used. He said the later ones are better. I said that I wanted to make sure that whoever looked at those paintings knew that she had had help. I asked, 'Is the information on file?' He said it was but not available for me to see. He suggested I write a letter to her, stating as unemotionally as possible what I wanted, and to send it by registered mail."

But Poling said he did not feel the letter would make the information widely available, and that he believed he must make it public in another way. It was then that several interviews with *The Santa Fe Reporter* were arranged.

Less than a week later, in her Ghost Ranch home, O'Keeffe, too, recalled that summer of 1976. Dressed in a blue cotton dress and a black smock, O'Keeffe sat against the wall of her study, the same study where Poling had worked with her, and chatted courteously about her present work.

When asked about Poling, however, her words turned spare and bitter. She confirmed that the painting which has been called informally The Patio and the two called *From a Day with Juan* were painted by Poling, although conceived and designed by her. But she stressed that his contribution had no artistic significance.

"Mr. Poling was the equivalent of a palette knife," she said. "He was nothing but a tool.... Since the beginning of time, artists have had assistants.... He (Poling) is just a troublemaker. He wants to make himself important at my expense.

"He wasn't any more useful than a brush," O'Keeffe said. "You have to have a brush, don't you? Is he anything but a tool if he does what I tell him to do? He had no thought, no part in the painting except that he could do what I told him to do."

O'Keeffe pointed to a sculpture about three feet high, first cast several decades ago, that she now plans to recast 10 feet high. "Am I to advertise the foundry that did this sculpture?" she said.

Asked about the patio painting, the first of the three, O'Keeffe said the painting had spoiled because of a technical problem. "That painting has to be destroyed. Something has gone wrong with it." Later, Hamilton explained that the paint had buckled on the canvas. Both he and O'Keeffe said it had never been shown beyond her homes, or put on the market.

Speaking of the other two paintings, O'Keeffe said neither of them was up for sale either. "I am not going to show the pictures. They are not on the market. If he thinks he is going to ride in on them, I'll just cut them up. I'm so disgusted with him.

"He was in my home, working, doing certain things," O'Keeffe said. "He wouldn't come to work on time. One time I asked him to move some wood. He said he wasn't willing to do anything but paint. I said, 'Well then, you'd better go home.'"

Asked whether she might comply with Poling's request to let people know that she had been assisted with three paintings, O'Keeffe said she would not: "I don't think it's anyone's business."

Hamilton, who joined the interview at this point, agreed with O'Keeffe on this question. "Does a translator have to give credit to his secretaries?" he asked. "Does a film maker describe what he edits out of his films? Why don't people ask me about my assistants with my sculpture?"

The degree of assistance in O'Keeffe's work was not the public's business, he said, and would always be "subject to interpretation."

Speaking of his conversation with Poling, Hamilton confirmed that he had asked him to write a letter to O'Keeffe stating his view of the facts, and had said that the letter would be added to O'Keeffe documents at Yale's Beinecke Library.

"I asked him to write a letter, and said it would go into the Beinecke file at Yale. Why does he do this now? Why didn't he express those feelings then?" Hamilton asked.

Hamilton said that one of the gray and blue paintings that Poling assisted O'Keeffe with has been shown in an exhibit at Buffalo's Albright-Knox Art Gallery. The exhibit was entitled *American Painting of the 1970s,* and was displayed in cities in California, Texas, Illinois and Ohio in late 1978 and 1979. Hamilton said he and O'Keeffe had found a very fine frame that fit the painting exactly, and that that was the main reason they had included it in the show.

Suddenly, O'Keeffe interrupted him, stating with slow and careful emphasis, "It *is* my painting."

"Of course it is," Hamilton assured her.

Incidents of O'Keeffe's using assistance are nothing new, and have been noted before—by the artist herself, Hamilton said. As an example, he referred to the massive 1976 Viking Press retrospective of her work, with a text written by O'Keeffe. In the book, she refers to a Frank Martinez who she says helped her mix paints for the huge 96-by-288-inch *Sky Above Clouds* canvas that she painted in 1966.

"It's obvious that if you're in your 70s, you need help in some ways," Hamilton said. He also referred to French painter Henri Matisse as another artist who, when elderly and bedridden, had cut out paper shapes that others placed on canvases. Yet no mention is made of his assistants, Hamilton said.

The interview at Ghost Ranch was not all somber, though. It broke into a lighter tone when Hamilton shifted the subject to announce that he had recently married, and that his bride was not O'Keeffe.

"Now, that rumor has no more room to expand," he quipped, while O'Keeffe smiled. Numerous rumors that the two were married had circulated in the past several years. Hamilton said he was married May 22.

A few days later, in a telephone interview, Hamilton discussed O'Keeffe's artistic output since her eyesight faded. Since then, she has completed about 20 or 30 watercolors a year without any assistance, and several have been sold, he said. Most of the watercolors are of simple designs and easier to execute than some of oils. She has also done a few pastels and charcoals, Hamilton said.

Hamilton said that in 1972, O'Keeffe lost part of her central vision, but not her peripheral vision. This means that objects look "cloudy" to her, and colors have paled, he said. "She tends to say it's getting worse, but I don't think so," he added.

He said it was incorrect that O'Keeffe only started in oils in 1976, as stated in *ARTnews*. Hamilton said that as early as 1973, she attempted "a rock painting" that was "unsuccessful." Then there were several more oils before Poling started with her on the seven-foot patio canvas, he said. Since Poling left, another four to six of the gray and blue series called *From a Day with Juan* have been completed, he said.

Asked about O'Keeffe's work before the 1970s, Hamilton said that to his knowledge, she had done her works entirely on her own, except in cases that presented unusual problems, such as murals or abnormally large canvases.

Hamilton said he thought that the most important thing was to encourage O'Keeffe to keep working. "Everyone knows about her eyesight," he said. "We tried to keep it quiet for a while because of her pride. She stopped painting for approximately a year. I encouraged her to start again. First there was a rock painting that was not successful. When John came, she was trying to do something she had an idea for. She worked with John because he had not studied art. He had no background in art. She would not work with anyone that had any ideas in his head.

"Since then, she has gotten involved in brushwork again," Hamilton said. "She just lets someone do the background areas. Never, since then, have I seen anyone execute an entire painting.

"No pictures that anyone else worked on have been sold, and only one was exhibited," Hamilton said. "That was a sad mistake—to have exhibited a picture that John painted. It won't be repeated."

Hamilton said O'Keeffe still had many ideas for paintings, and that everyone in the household assisted her in small ways. "The whole idea is," he paused to underline his words, "that she should keep on painting."

Appendix D

Yale University Library,
1603A Yale Station
New Haven, Connecticut 06520

November 20, 1984

I gratefully acknowledge the receipt of the gift mentioned below and extend to you

our sincere thanks.

Faithfully yours,

Jack A. Siggins
Deputy University Librarian

For the Yale Collection of American
Literature, The Beinecke Rare Book
and Manuscript Library:

The Sante Fe reporter: a weekly
    journal. City edition. Sante
    Fe, 1980. Vol. 7, no. 6, July
    31, 1980.
    Contains article about Georgia O'Keeffe

To Mr. John Poling
      83B Bishop Street
      New Haven, Connecticut   06511

Selected Bibliography

A. By and About O'Keeffe

Aldrich, Hope. "Art Assist: Where is Credit Due?" and "Truth Vital, Experts Say." *The Santa Fe Reporter,* vol. 7, no. 6, 31 July, 1980.

Asbury, Edith Evans. "Silent Desert Still Charms Georgia O'Keeffe, Near 81." *New York Times,* 2 November 1968.

Cowart, Jack, and Hamilton, Juan. *Georgia O'Keeffe: Art and Letters.* Washington, D.C.: National Gallery of Art, in association with New York Graphic Society Books, 1987.

Fisk University, Nashville, Tennessee. The Carl Van Vechten Gallery of Fine Arts. Catalogue: *The Alfred Stieglitz Collection for Fisk University,* n.d. "Foreword" by Georgia O'Keeffe; "The Alfred Stieglitz Collection for Fisk University" by Charles S. Johnson; "Introduction" by Carl Zigrosser.

————. *The Alfred Stieglitz Collection for Fisk University,* 1984. "Foreword" by David C. Driskell; "Introduction" by Robert L. Hall.

Giboire, Clive, ed. *Lovingly, Georgia. The Complete Correspondence of Georgia O'Keeffe and Anita Pollitzer.* New York: Touchstone, 1990.

Hogrefe, Jeffrey. *O'Keeffe: The Life of an American Legend.* New York: Bantam, 1992.

Kotz, Mary Lynn. "A Day with Georgia O'Keeffe." *ARTnews,* vol. 76, no. 10, December 1977.

Lopez, Judy. "An Interview with Georgia O'Keeffe." *El Fogon.* Española: University of New Mexico, Northern Branch College, vol. 1, Spring 1977.

Lynes, Barbara Buhler. *O'Keeffe, Stieglitz and the Critics, 1916-1929.* Chicago: The University of Chicago Press, 1989.

Moore, James. "So Clear Cut Where the Sun Will Come . . . : Georgia O'Keeffe's 'Gray Cross With Blue'." *ARTSPACE: Southwestern Contemporary Arts Quarterly,* vol. 10, no. 3, Summer 1986.

Merrill, Christopher, and Bradbury, Ellen, eds. *From The Faraway Nearby. Georgia O'Keeffe as Icon.* Reading, Mass.: Addison-Wesley Press, 1992.

O'Keeffe, Georgia. *Georgia O'Keeffe.* New York: The Viking Press/Penguin Books, 1976.

————. "Introduction." *Georgia O'Keeffe: A Portrait by Alfred Stieglitz.* By Alfred Stieglitz. New York: Metropolitan Museum of Art, 1978.

———. *Some Memories of Drawings*. Edited by Doris Bry. Albuquerque: University of New Mexico Press, 1974.

Patten, Christine Taylor, and Cardona-Hine, Alvaro. *Miss O'Keeffe*. Albuquerque: University of New Mexico Press, 1992.

Robinson, Roxana. *Georgia O'Keeffe: A Life*. New York: Harper & Row, 1989.

B. Related Works

Aldrich, Virgil C. *Philosophy of Art*. Englewood Cliffs, N.J.: Prentice-Hall, 1963.

Best, David. *Feeling and Reason in the Arts*. London: George Allen & Unwin, Ltd., 1985.

Brown, Francis, ed. *Opinions and Perspectives from the New York Times Book Review*. Boston: Houghton Mifflin Co., 1964.

———. *Page 2: The Best of "Speaking of Books" from the New York Times Book Review*. New York: Holt, Rinehart and Winston, 1969.

Cather, Willa. *Not Under Forty*. New York: Alfred A. Knopf, 1936.

———. "On Various Minor Painters." In *Writers on Artists*. Edited by Daniel Halpern. San Francisco: North Point Press, 1988.

———. *On Writing*. New York: Alfred A. Knopf, 1949.

Doerner, Max. *The Materials of the Artist and Their Use in Painting; With Notes on the Techniques of the Old Masters*. Trans. by Eugen Neuhaus. New York: Harcourt, Brace and Co., 1934.

Holmer, Paul L. *C. S. Lewis: The Shape of His Faith and Thought*. New York: Harper & Row, 1976.

———. *The Grammar of Faith*. New York: Harper & Row, 1978.

Horgan, Paul. *A Certain Climate: Essays in History, Arts, and Letters*. Middletown, Conn.: Wesleyan University Press, 1988.

Kuh, Katherine. *The Artist's Voice*. New York: Harper & Row, 1962.

Lewis, C. S. *The Abolition of Man*. New York: Macmillan, 1947.

———. *An Experiment in Criticism*. Cambridge: Cambridge University Press, 1961.

———. *On Stories*. Edited by Walter Hooper. New York: Harcourt, Brace, Jovanovich, 1982.

MacIntyre, Alasdair. *After Virtue*. Notre Dame: University of Notre Dame Press, 1981.

Rhees, Rush. *Without Answers*. New York: Schocken Books, 1969.

Wilder, Thornton. *American Characteristics*. Edited by Donald Gallup. New York: Harper & Row, 1979.

Winch, Peter. *Trying to Make Sense*. Oxford: Basil Blackwell Ltd., 1987.

Wittgenstein, Ludwig. *Culture and Value*. Edited by G. H. von Wright. Translated by Peter Winch. Chicago: University of Chicago Press, 1980.

———. *Lectures and Conversations*. Edited by Cyril Barrett. Berkeley: University of California Press, n.d.

———. *Philosophical Investigations.* Third edition. Translated by G. E. M. Anscombe. New York: Macmillan Publishing Co., Inc., 1958.

———. *Zettel.* Edited by G. E. M. Anscombe & G. H. von Wright. Translated by G. E. M. Anscombe. Berkeley: University of California Press, 1967.

Wren, Linnea H. "John LaFarge, Aesthetician and Critic," in *John LaFarge: Essays,* by Henry Adams, *et. al.* New York: Abbeville Press, 1987.

Index

A

Abiquiu, viii, xi, 1, 3–4, 7, 10, 14–18, 20–22, 27–29
Abiquiu Dam, 1, 8, 47, 103
Abiquiu Mesa, 12, 29
Adato, Perry Miller, 28, 37
Albright-Knox Gallery in Buffalo, 115
Albuquerque, New Mexico, 2, 3, 8, 18–19, 81
Aldrich, Hope, xv, 113, 133, 136–148
American Painting of the 1970s, 115
Angkor Wat, 51
Archuleta, Ida, 27, 38, 50, 73, 92
"Art Assist: Where Is Credit Due?" 114, Appendix C
ARTnews magazine, 101–102, 107, 110, 112, 115, 116
Arts Students League, vii
Asbury, Edith Evans, 117

B

Barranco, New Mexico, xi, 1–2, 5, 8, 10, 21, 29
Beinecke Rare Book and Manuscript Library at Yale, 44, 112
Bement, Alon, 127
Benedictine Monastery of Christ in the Desert, 46
Black Rock, 28
Black Market, 49
Black Mountain Range, 3
Bode's General Store, 1, 2, 16
Bry, Doris, 9, 50

C

Calder, Alexander, 35
Camera Work, 80
Cañon del Cobre, 5, 12
Cañones, New Mexico, 32, 108, 113
Chama River, 1, 6, 8, 10, 13, 46
Chase, William Merritt, vii
Chimayo, New Mexico, 11
Chimney Rock, 23
Claremont Graduate School in California, 9
Conjectures of a Guilty Bystander, 46
Costa Rica, 9
Crosby, John, 51–52

D

Day with Juan, xi, 100, 102, 115–116
"Day with Georgia O'Keeffe," 107
Dow, Arthur Wesley, vii

E

El Rito Mountain, 29
Eldredge, Charles, viii
Española, New Mexico, 1, 15–16, 51

F

Fields, Mrs. Annie Adams, 118
Fisk University, 129
From the Faraway Nearby, 124

G

Gallina Canyon, 46
Georgia O'Keeffe: A Life, 115
Ghost Ranch Conference Center, 2, 3–4, 7, 9–10, 15–16, 27, 81, 93
Grether, Mary, 1, 5, 10, 18–19, 30–33, 35, 37, 50, 53, 57–59, 66, 73

H

Hall, Jim, 9, 27
Hall, Ruth and Jim, 10
Hamilton, Juan (John Bruce), viii, 8, 9–10, 12–13, 14, 16–19, 31, 64, 71, 81–82, 86–91, 100, 103, 107, 112, 115, 118
Harrill, James, xv, 10, 108, 113
Hastings College in Nebraska, 9
Hidden Remnant, The, 48
Hillsboro, New Mexico, 3

I

Inca, 31

J

Jemez Mountains, 19, 51
Jingo, 31
Jones, Gallegos, Snead, and Wertheim, xvi, 115–116

K

Katz, Bill, 51
Kempes, Jim, 4, 7, 10, 11, 12, 14, 40, 43, 78, 103

L

La Bajada Hill, 19
Lachaise, Gaston, 77
Lawrence, D. H., 80
Lopez, Candelaria or "Candy," 17, 27, 31
Lopez, Pita, 53
Lujan, Mabel Dodge, 80

M

Machu Picchu, 51
Materials of the Artist, The, 92
McKinney, Louise, 44, 47
McKinney, Robin, 44, 47
Merton, Thomas, 46
Mesa Montosa, 7, 54
Morocco, 9
Mother of Us All, The, 49

N

New Mexico Magazine, 44
New Republic, The, 40
New York, 14, 16, 31
New York City, vii
New York Times, The, 117
Newsweek, 114

O

O'Keeffe Foundation, 115
O'Keeffe's sister Claudia, 30, 48
Oseid, Jane, 93, 104
Owen, Aubrey, 81

P

The Patio or Patio Door, xi, 10, 27, 101, 115–116

Pack, Arthur and Phoebe, 3
Pedernal, 7–8, 22, 32, 51, 71
Phelps, Steve, 117
Poling, Leslie Eliot, xvii, 10
Poling-Kempes, Lesley, 4, 10, 12, 43, 78
Pollitzer, Anita, 120, 128
Project HOPE ship nurses, 51

R

Rancho de Chimayo, 11, 14
Rancho de los Brujos, or Ranch of the Witches, 3
Rio Arriba County, 2

Rio Grande, 19
Robinson, Roxana, 115
Rose, Barbara, viii, 28

S

San Juan Pueblo, 52
Sandia Mountains, 19
Sangre de Cristo Mountains, 19,
    50–51
Santa Fe, New Mexico, xvi, 1, 19–20,
    30, 48, 50–51, 114
Santa Fe Opera, 49, 51
Santa Fe Reporter, The, 113–114
Seth, Jean and Oliver, 86
Smythers, John, 50
South America, 9, 14
St. Olaf College, viii, xvi
Starlight Night, 29
Stieglitz, Alfred, vii, 52, 80, 129
Stieglitz/O'Keeffe archives, 44, 129
Suazo, Esteban, "old Steven," 17
Suazo, Steven, 17, 31
Sun Prairie, Wisconsin, vii
Sykes, Gerald, 48, 50

T

Taos, 29
Teacher's College, Columbia University, vii

Ted, 13–14, 16
Ticknor and Fields, 118
Truth or Consequences, New Mexico, 3
"Truth Vital, Experts Say," 114, Appendix C

U

University of New Mexico, 3
University of Virginia, 127

V

Vanderbilt University, 129
Vietnam War, 10
Viking Press, 9, 16

W

Washington Monument, 100
Washington, D. C., 91
Weather Report, 49
Webster and Sheffield, 50
Wells, Cady, 119
Westchester County in New York, 2
White Patio with Red Door, 68
Wittgenstein, Ludwig, 121–23, 126
Wooster, College of, 2, 3

Y

Yale Divinity School, 4, 8, 117